Sight-Reading for CONTEMPORARY GUITARIST

THE ULTIMATE GUIDE TO MUSIC FOR BLUES, ROCK AND JAZZ GUITARISTS

Tom Dempsey

Alfred, the leader in educational publishing, and the National Guitar Workshop, one of America's finest guitar schools, have joined forces to bring you the best, most progressive educational tools possible. We hope you will enjoy this book and encourage you to look for other fine products from Alfred and the National Guitar Workshop.

This book was acquired, edited and produced by Workshop Arts, Inc., the publishing arm of the National Guitar Workshop.
Nathaniel Gunod: acquisitions, managing editor
Michael Rodman: editor
Matt Cramer: music typesetter and assistant editor
Timothy Phelps: interior design

Cover photos: Jeff Oshiro
Cover models (left to right, top to bottom):
Matt Simmons, Link Harnsberger,
Martha Widmann, Marta Csotsits, Ron Manus

Copyright © MMIII by Alfred Publishing Co., Inc.
All rights reserved. Printed in USA.

ISBN 0-7390-3156-2

Table of Contents

About the Author 4

Introduction 4

CHAPTER 1—REVIEW OF MUSICAL BASICS 6
Pitch 6
Time 7

CHAPTER 2—READING RHYTHMS 10
Counting Rhythms 10
Rhythmic Pattern Repertoire 12
The Complete Fretboard 14
Notes on Each String 16
Single-String Reading Exercises 18

CHAPTER 3—POSITION READING, C MAJOR 20
Octave Shapes 20
Major Scale Shapes 20
Positions on the Guitar 21
C Major Scale Positions 22
C Major Exercises 23
Reading Intervals and Triads 26
C Major Harmonic Reading Exercises 28

CHAPTER 4—G MAJOR READING EXERCISES 29
G Major Scale Positions 29
G Major Exercises 30
G Major Harmonic Reading Exercises 33

CHAPTER 5—F MAJOR READING EXERCISES 34
F Major Scale Positions 34
F Major Exercises 35
F Major Harmonic Reading Exercises 38

CHAPTER 6—D MAJOR READING EXERCISES 39
D Major Scale Positions 39
D Major Exercises 40
D Major Harmonic Reading Exercises 43

CHAPTER 7—B♭ MAJOR READING EXERCISES 44
B♭ Major Scale Positions 44
B♭ Major Exercises 45
B♭ Major Harmonic Reading Exercises 48

CHAPTER 8—A MAJOR READING EXERCISES 49
A Major Scale Positions 49
A Major Exercises 50
A Major Harmonic Reading Exercises 53

CHAPTER 9—E♭ MAJOR READING EXERCISES 54
E♭ Major Scale Positions 54
E♭ Major Exercises 55
E♭ Major Harmonic Reading Exercises 58

Chapter 10—E Major Reading Exercises 59
E Major Scale Positions 59
E Major Exercises 60
E Major Harmonic Reading Exercises 63

Chapter 11—A♭ Major Reading Exercises 64
A♭ Major Scale Positions 64
A♭ Major Exercises 65
A♭ Major Harmonic Reading Exercises 68

Chapter 12—B Major Reading Exercises 69
B Major Scale Positions 69
B Major Exercises 70
B Major Harmonic Reading Exercises 73

Chapter 13—D♭ Major Reading Exercises 74
D♭ Major Scale Positions 74
D♭ Major Exercises 75
D♭ Major Harmonic Reading Exercises 78

Chapter 14—F# Major Reading Exercises 79
F# Major Scale Positions 79
F# Major Exercises 80
F# Major Harmonic Reading Exercises 83

Chapter 15—G♭ Major Reading Exercises 84
G♭ Major Scale Positions 84
G♭ Major Exercises 85
G♭ Major Harmonic Reading Exercises 88

Chapter 16—C# Major Reading Exercises 89
C# Major Scale Positions 89
C# Major Exercises 90
C# Major Harmonic Reading Exercises 93

Chapter 17—C♭ Major Reading Exercises 94
C♭ Major Scale Positions 94
C♭ Major Exercises 95
C♭ Major Harmonic Reading Exercises 98

Chapter 18—More Multi-Position Reading 99

Chapter 19—Reading in Odd Time 104

Chapter 20—Chord Chart Reading Exercises 107

The Final Bar 111

About the Author

For more than ten years, Tom Dempsey has received widespread acclaim for his excellence, sophistication and artistry in the New York jazz scene. Tom has performed and/or recorded with a virtual "Who's Who" of the jazz world, including Jim Hall, John Abercrombie, John Scofield, Tal Farlow, Buddy Montgomery, George Coleman, Kenny Barron, Roy Haynes, Jack McDuff, Gerald Wilson, Mel Torme, Richard Wyands, Muhal Richard Abrams and Dave Brubeck. Since 1992, Tom has performed as a leader and sideman at top jazz venues throughout the United States, Europe and Japan. He has made numerous appearances on radio and television, including performances on *The Rosie O'Donnell Show*, the HBO series *Sex and the City* and radio station WQXR. His CD *Blues in the Slope* (Igmod) has received critical acclaim. Tom is an Artist Endorsee for Yamaha Guitars and for J. Demonte Guitars of Buenos Aires, Argentina.

Tom's deep commitment to education has made him a highly sought-after educator and clinician. He has taught in the Jazz Studies program at SUNY New Paltz and is the Director of the Jazz Summit at the National Guitar Workshop. His book *Guitar Styles: Classic Jazz* is available from Workshop Arts and Alfred Publishing.

DEDICATION

This book is dedicated in loving memory to Ted Dunbar (1937–1998).

"Just keep on going straight ahead."—Ted Dunbar

ACKNOWLEDGMENTS

Very special thanks to David and Barbara Smolover for the creation of the National Guitar Workshop, which has played and continues to play an integral role in my development as a musician; to Nat Gunod and Michael Rodman for their patience and guidance throughout the development of this book; to Ted Dunbar, who taught me as a young guitarist to strive for the highest level of musicianship possible; and to Rodney Jones, who continues to inspire me through his music, teaching and example to raise the bar in my musicianship and artistry. I am forever grateful for all that you have shared with me.

Introduction

The goal of this book is to help guitarists who already know how to read music become proficient sight-readers. The term *sight-reading* refers to the act of playing a piece of music at first sight—without previous rehearsal. To get the most out of this book, you should already be a fairly good reader in the open position (the open strings and the first four frets). This book will help you become a good reader throughout the full range of the fretboard, in all keys.

Some of the requirements for becoming a good sight-reader are:
- A good understanding of music theory
- A complete knowledge of the guitar fretboard
- A good musical "ear"

Great sight-readers make reading look easy because their deep knowledge of their instrument, musical style and theory—plus the clarity with which they hear what is happening in the music—allow them to know what to expect to see in the written music. Therefore, this book is best used in conjunction with the other books in this series, or others like them:

Ear Training for the Contemporary Guitarist
Fretboard for the Contemporary Guitarist
Theory for the Contemporary Guitarist

When I was first learning to play guitar, one of my staples for the bus ride home from school was *Guitar Player* magazine. Like most adolescent guitar players of the time, I was in awe of the brilliant talent that plastered the pages of this periodical. One column that always caught my eye was written by the legendary studio guitarist Tommy Tedesco. Every month, Tommy went through one of his countless studio sessions. I thought it was interesting that he was able to play in so many diverse musical settings. One reason that people called on him so often was that his sight-reading skills were excellent.

Sight-reading became of paramount importance to me as I went through school and performed with different ensembles. The sight-reading experience I gained in these different settings carried over into my professional career. Today, I enjoy the freedom to perform in a number of different settings, which has greatly enriched my career and the breadth of my musicianship. The main factor in affording me these opportunities has been my ability to read music.

Reading music on the guitar can be challenging. For example, a single note can be played in five (or even more) different places on the instrument. The fact that we need to be able to read not only single notes but also melodic lines, counterpoint, chords and chord charts doesn't make our job any easier. And then there is the issue of position choices. It's no wonder that guitarists are the butt of so many sight-reading jokes. If you're still scared, join the club—but also know that reading music for the guitar is far from impossible.

This book attempts to present a clear methodology for learning how to sight-read. If you're thorough in your approach to studying this text, the sight-reading stumbling blocks you may have faced in the past will melt away. The first section reviews the basic elements of music as they relate to sight-reading. If you feel secure in your knowledge of the basics, feel free to skip to the second section, which deals with reading on single strings and position playing in different keys. When practicing the exercises, be sure to follow the directions, including the indications for position/location on the neck of the guitar. Once you've mastered the exercises as presented, many of them can be transposed up an octave. This is a good skill to develop, since the guitar sounds an octave lower than written. Guitarists are also often asked to transpose at sight. The reading examples provide excellent material for practicing this skill.

The third section of the book covers multi-position playing. Here, you'll work on pieces that move beyond one position on the guitar. From there, you'll progress to playing in odd time signatures and reading chord charts.

Don't be in a hurry to get through the book; the idea isn't to finish as quickly as possible, but to be thorough and to build lasting skills. You may reach a point at which you feel that you're just memorizing the examples. That's okay; the main thing to keep in mind is to be consistently looking at the music as you play. What you're doing is training your eyes, hands and brain to work together so that the reading process becomes natural.

Chapter 1 – Review of Musical Basics

PITCH

NOTES
Music is written by placing notes on a *staff*. Notes appear in various forms.

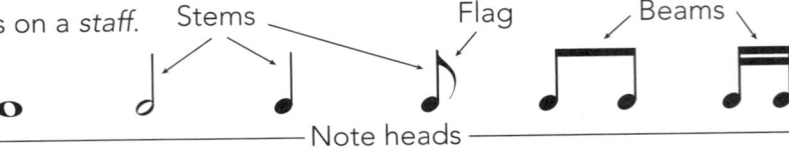

THE STAFF AND CLEF

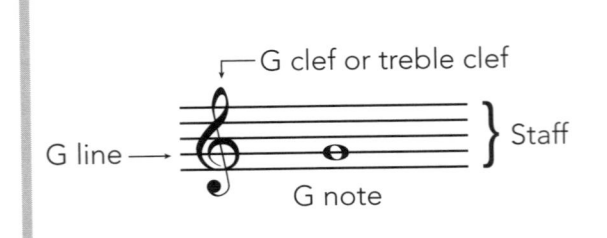

The staff has five lines and four spaces and is read from left to right. At the beginning of the staff is a *clef*. The clef dictates what note corresponds to a particular line or space on the staff. Guitar music is written in *treble clef* 𝄞, which is sometimes called the *G clef*. The ending curl of the clef encircles the G line on the staff.

Here are the notes on the staff using the G clef:

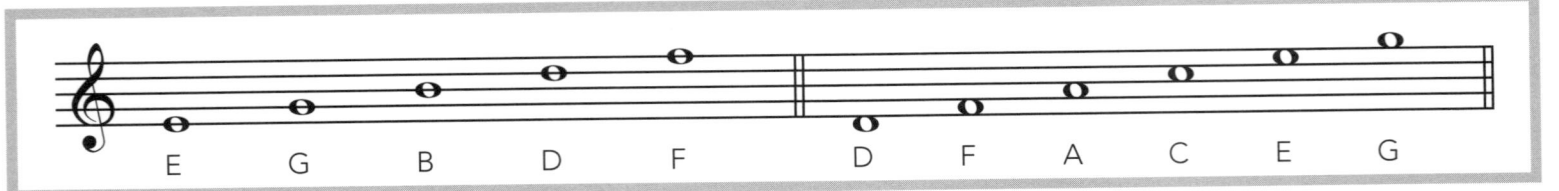

E G B D F | D F A C E G

ACCIDENTALS
Signs called *accidentals* change the pitch of a note. A *flat* (♭) lowers the pitch of a note by a half step.

D   D♭

A *sharp* (♯) raises the pitch of a note by a half step.

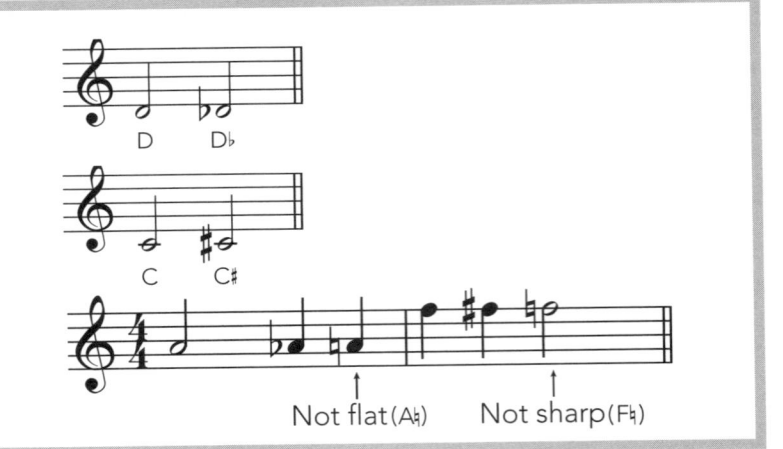

C   C♯

Both flats and sharps apply only to the exact line and space in which they appear. A *natural* (♮) cancels a flat or sharp.

Not flat (A♮)   Not sharp (F♮)

LEDGER LINES
The higher a note appears on the staff, the higher it sounds. When a note is too high or too low to be written on the staff, *ledger lines* are used.

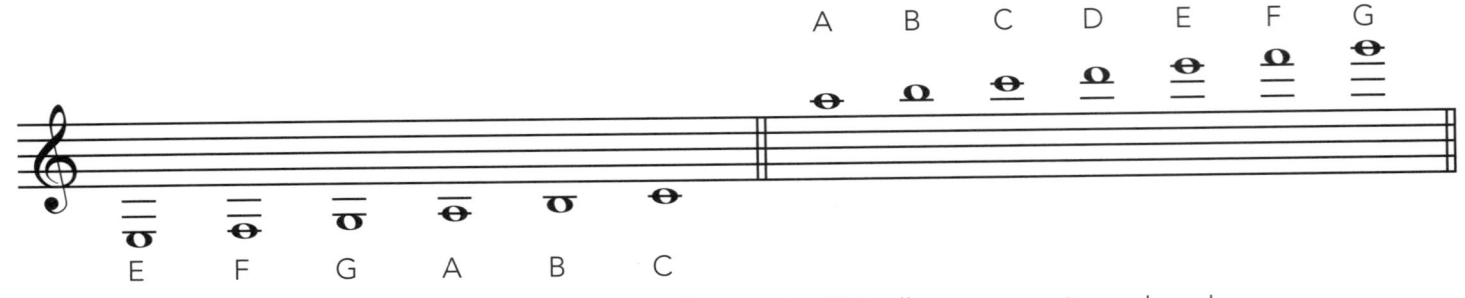

A B C D E F G

E F G A B C

Guitar music is written one octave higher than it actually sounds. This allows us to write and read music on one clef, instead of using two clefs as with keyboard instruments.

Time

Measures and Bar Lines

The staff is divided by vertical lines called *bar lines*. The space between two bar lines is called a *measure*. Measures divide music into groups of *beats*. A beat is an equal division of time. Beats are the basic pulse behind music. A *double bar* marks the end of a section or example.

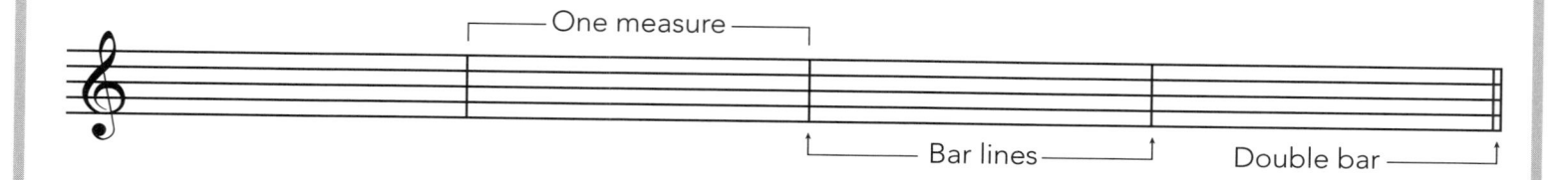

Note and Rest Values

As you know, the location of a note on the staff tells us its pitch (how high or how low it is). The duration, or value, is indicated by its shape. Every note has a corresponding *rest*, which indicates silence.

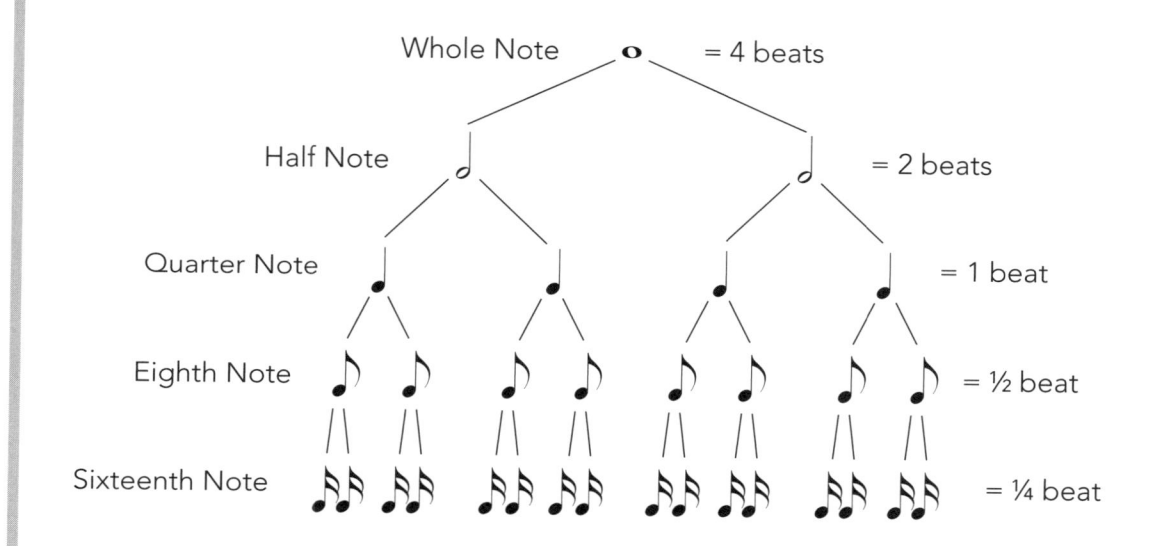

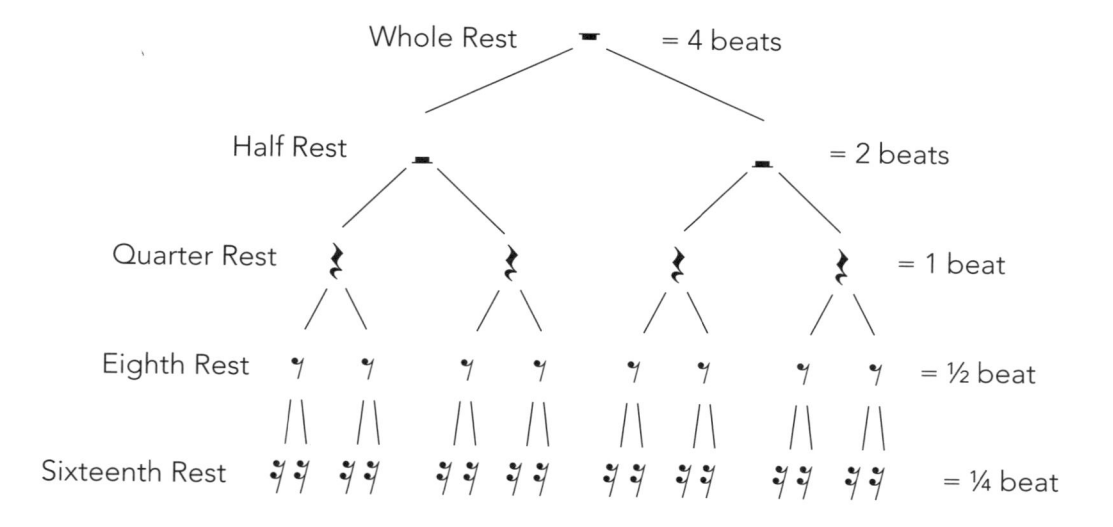

Whole Note	= 4 beats
Half Note	= 2 beats
Quarter Note	= 1 beat
Eighth Note	= ½ beat
Sixteenth Note	= ¼ beat

Whole Rest	= 4 beats
Half Rest	= 2 beats
Quarter Rest	= 1 beat
Eighth Rest	= ½ beat
Sixteenth Rest	= ¼ beat

Time Signatures

Every piece of music has a pair of numbers at the beginning called a *time signature* that tell us how to count time. The top number represents the number of beats per measure. The bottom number represents the type of note receiving one beat. Time signatures with 2, 3 or 4 as the top number are called *simple* time signatures.

4/4   4 beats per measure
       Quarter note ♩ = one beat

3/4   3 beats per measure
       Quarter note ♩ = one beat

Sometimes a **C** is used in place of 4/4. This is called *common time*.

2/2 or ¢   2 beats per measure
          Half note 𝅗𝅥 = one beat

This is also called *cut time*.

Time signatures in which the upper number is a multiple of 3 (aside from 3 itself) are called *compound* time signatures. Commonly used compound time signatures include 6/8, 9/8 and 12/8. Music in compound time is often felt and counted differently than music in simple time. In a measure of 6/8, for example, the eighth note still receives one beat, but the feel of the music may actually suggest two groups of three eighth notes, counted like this:

     1   &   a   2   &   a

This same principle also applies to other compound time signatures.

Ties

When notes are *tied*, the second note is not struck. Rather, its value is added to that of the first note. So, a half note tied to a quarter note equals three beats.

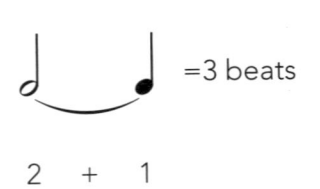

𝅗𝅥 ♩ = 3 beats
2 + 1

Notice the numbers under the staff in these examples. They indicate how to count. Both of these examples are in 4/4 time, so we count four beats in each measure. When there are eighth notes, which are only half a beat, we count "&" ("and") to show the division of the beat into two parts. When a counting number is in parentheses, that note is being held rather than struck.

Ties are a convenient way to notate notes that begin off the beat (on an "&").

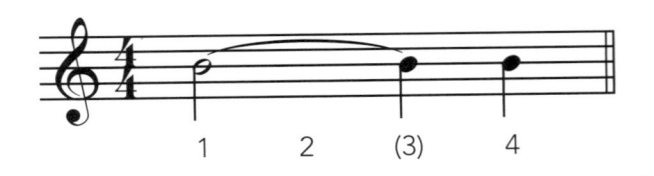

     1   2   &   (3)   &   4

     1   2   (3)   4

Dots

A dot increases the length of a note by one half of its original value. For instance, a half note equals two beats. Half of its value is one beat (a quarter note). So a dotted half note equals three beats (2 + 1 = 3). A dotted half note is equal to a half note tied to a quarter note.

𝅗𝅥 ♩ = 𝅗𝅥.   ♩ ♪ = ♩.   ♪ 𝅘𝅥𝅯 = ♪.
2 + 1 = 3   1 + ½ = 1½   ½ + ¼ = ¾

Dotted notes are especially important when the time signature is 3/4, because the longest note value that will fit in a measure is a dotted half note. Dotted notes are also very important in 6/8 time. Not only is a dotted half note the longest possible note value, but a dotted quarter note is exactly half of a measure (counted 1 & a 2 & a).

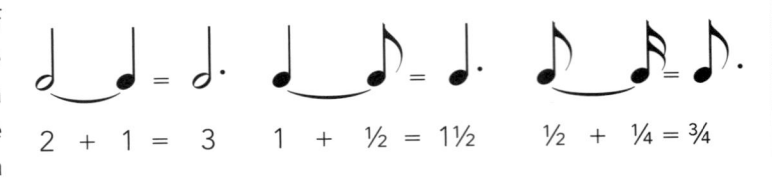

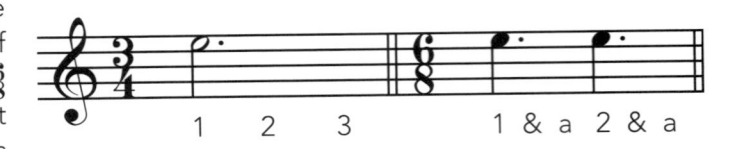

     1   2   3   1 & a 2 & a

Triplets

A *triplet* is a group of three notes that divides beats or parts of beats into three equal parts.

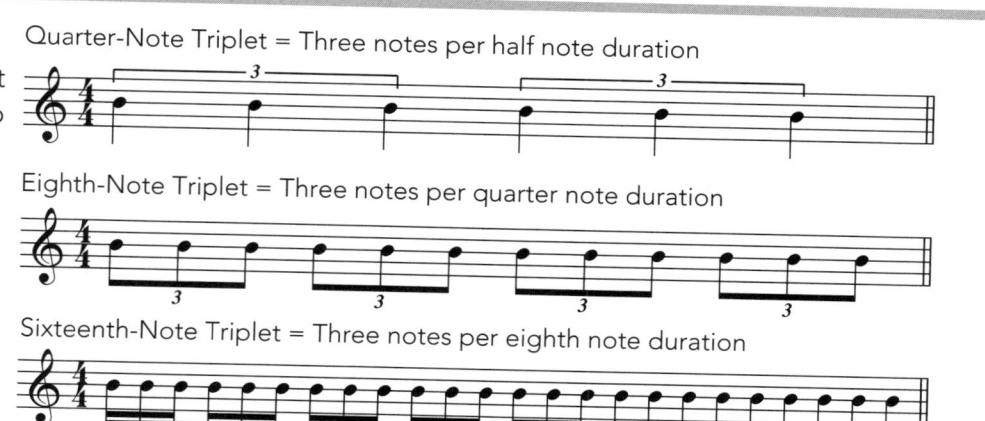

Quarter-Note Triplet = Three notes per half note duration

Eighth-Note Triplet = Three notes per quarter note duration

Sixteenth-Note Triplet = Three notes per eighth note duration

Beaming

Notes that are less than one quarter note in duration are often *beamed* together. Notice the counting numbers: Since there are four sixteenth notes in a beat, they are counted "1 e & a 2 e & a," etc.

Beamed sixteenth notes

1 e & a 2 e & a

Beamed eighth notes

1 & 2 & 3 & 4 &

Key Signatures

At right are all the key signatures, major and minor, that we'll use throughout the book. Memorizing these key signatures will aid you in becoming a strong sight-reader.

A more detailed explanation of key signatures can be found in *Theory for the Contemporary Guitarist*, which will give you an overview of this and other topics in this chapter.

C Major/A Minor

G Major/E Minor
E Major/C# Minor
F Major/D Minor
A♭ Major/F Minor

D Major/B Minor
B Major/G# Minor
B♭ Major/G Minor
D♭ Major/B♭ Minor

A Major/F# Minor
F# Major/D# Minor
E♭ Major/C Minor
G♭ Major/E♭ Minor

C# Major/A# Minor
C♭ Major/A♭ Minor

Fretboard Diagrams

A *fretboard diagram* is a graphic representation of the neck of the guitar. Horizontal lines represent strings, and vertical lines represent frets. The frets are numbered below the diagram.

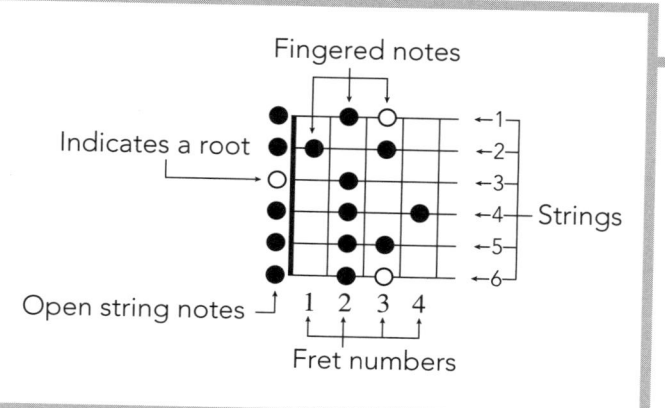

Fingered notes

Indicates a root

Strings

Open string notes

Fret numbers

Chapter 2—Reading Rhythms

One of the biggest challenges in becoming a good sight-reader is mastering rhythm. We must be able to recognize rhythmic patterns immediately and be able to perform them fluently with excellent adherence to the pulse.

You must develop a dependable inner *metronome* (an adjustable device that indicates the exact tempo of a piece), or what is often a called a "good sense of rhythm." A musician with this trait can easily establish a tempo and hold it, unerringly, throughout the length of entire composition. Common shortfalls in this ability are the tendency to drag (slow down) or rush (speed up).

Such problems can be trained out of your playing by consistent practice with a metronome. Practice without a metronome should be the exception rather than the rule. If you do not own a metronome, get one. When practicing a composition for performance, you should have a final tempo in mind, and work towards being able to play the piece at that speed. Choose practice tempos that challenge you but are sustainable. Practicing too quickly will lead to difficulty and error, which will then become habits.

It is worthwhile to spend time every day clapping or playing an open string with the clicks of the metronome at a variety of tempos. If you are clapping exactly with the clicks, you will not hear them well, if at all. If you do hear them clearly, you are probably clapping a little ahead of (before) the clicks or a little behind (after) them. It may be a challenge, but it behooves you to make sure you can master this skill.

Sight-reading, of course, is not really about practicing to perfection; it is about being able to perform music "on-sight," the first time you see it. At least 50 percent of the battle is being able to read the rhythm. This skill is developed in two steps:

1. Develop an efficient strategy for counting and understanding new rhythms when you see them.
2. Develop a large repertoire of rhythmic patterns that you immediately recognize and can easily perform.

COUNTING RHYTHMS

The age-old, proven method for counting rhythms is to spot the smallest rhythmic subdivision of the measure and verbalize it (until it is so internalized that verbalization is unnecessary), placing the performed notes exactly on the correct beats or parts of the beats.

Below are some suggestions for counting the most commonly used subdivisions. Practice counting all of them aloud with a metronome, striving to keep your counting perfectly even and exactly in sync with the clicks.

EXAMPLE 2.1: QUARTER NOTES

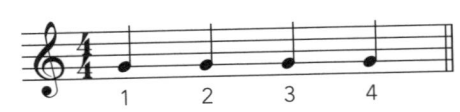

EXAMPLE 2.2: EIGHTH NOTES

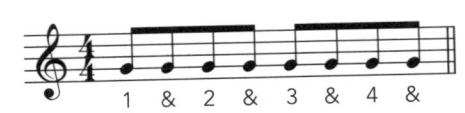

Sight-Reading for the Contemporary Guitarist

EXAMPLE 2.3: SIXTEENTH NOTES

1 e & a 2 e & a 3 e & a 4 e & a

EXAMPLE 2.4: EIGHTH-NOTE TRIPLETS

1 & a 2 & a 3 & a 4 & a

EXAMPLE 2.5: SIXTEENTH-NOTE TRIPLETS

1 trip-let & trip-let 2 trip-let & trip-let

Until the sense of dividing two beats (rather than one beat) into three parts is fully internalized, quarter-note triplets are most easily counted by subdividing them with eighth-note triplets.

EXAMPLE 2.6: QUARTER-NOTE TRIPLETS

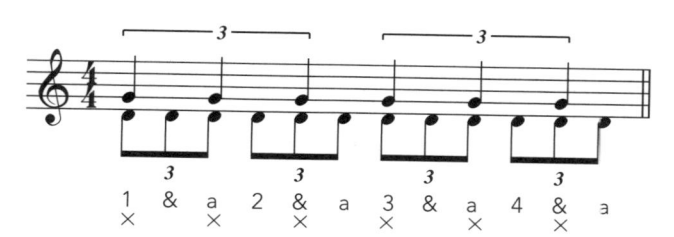

X = Clap Here

1 & a 2 & a 3 & a 4 & a

PREPARATORY BEATS AND SWITCHING SUBDIVISION

When applying these counting strategies, count the smallest subdivision in the measure for the entire measure, or at the very least, give yourself one full *preparatory beat* of counting the next subdivision that is needed. When counting subdivisions smaller than the actual notes, clap only where the notes fall.

EXAMPLE 2.7

1 2 3 4 & 1 & 2 & 3 & 4 e & a 1 e & a 2 e & a 3 e & a 4 e & a 1 2 3 4
——Preparatory beats——

Some of the most challenging situations occur when the subdivision changes from *simple* (divisible by two or four), as in eighth notes or sixteenth notes, to *compound* (divisible by three), such as triplets. One must have developed a sure sense of each of the two kinds of subdivision in order to easily switch between them. The second measure of Example 2.8 shows a common version of this situation.

EXAMPLE 2.8

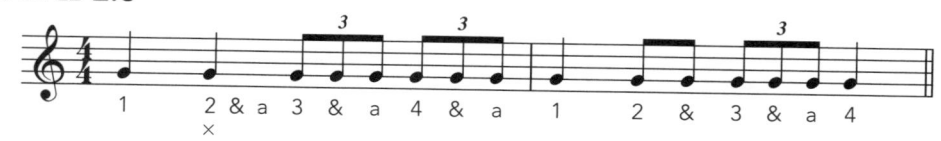

1 2 & a 3 & a 4 & a 1 2 & 3 & a 4

12 Sight-Reading for the Contemporary Guitarist

RHYTHMIC PATTERN REPERTOIRE

The many rhythmic patterns that follow by no means reflect all of the possible rhythm patterns available, or even every rhythmic pattern you'll encounter in this book, but learning them thoroughly will help prepare you for most rhythms you will ever encounter. Once your rhythmic vocabulary has a strong foundation, learning new rhythms becomes very easy; you will become able to perform new, unfamiliar rhythms on sight.

Make sure you have mastered every rhythm on this page, and are to play them all at a variety of tempos, from very slow to very fast, before continuing in this book. It is worth many weeks of study. Try writing the beat counts underneath. Clap each rhythm with a metronome set to quarter notes for the rhythms in $\frac{4}{4}$ and dotted quarter notes for those in $\frac{6}{8}$, repeating each until you've mastered it. Then, play each example on single strings; play various scales that you know in each rhythm; play the notes of favorite melodies in each—in other words, do everything you can think of to learn them thoroughly. And yes, you should learn to perform quarter-note triplets against a quarter-note click!

EXAMPLE 2.9

EXAMPLE 2.10

EXAMPLE 2.11

The Complete Fretboard

The diagram on these two pages shows the open and fretted notes on the guitar and how each note appears on the staff.

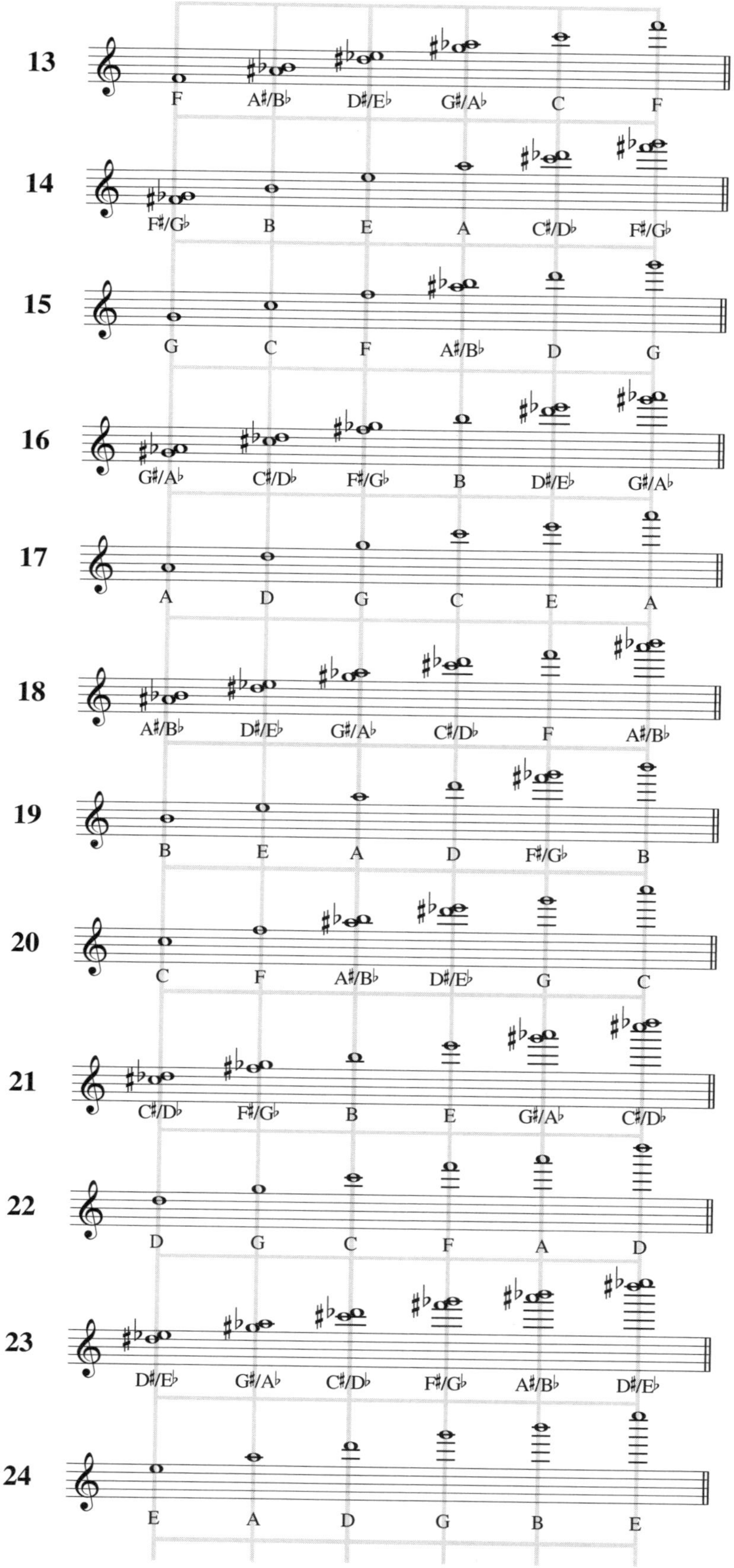
13
F A♯/B♭ D♯/E♭ G♯/A♭ C F
14
F♯/G♭ B E A C♯/D♭ F♯/G♭
15
G C F A♯/B♭ D G
16
G♯/A♭ C♯/D♭ F♯/G♭ B D♯/E♭ G♯/A♭
17
A D G C E A
18
A♯/B♭ D♯/E♭ G♯/A♭ C♯/D♭ F A♯/B♭
19
B E A D F♯/G♭ B
20
C F A♯/B♭ D♯/E♭ G C
21
C♯/D♭ F♯/G♭ B E G♯/A♭ C♯/D♭
22
D G C F A D
23
D♯/E♭ G♯/A♭ C♯/D♭ F♯/G♭ A♯/B♭ D♯/E♭
24
E A D G B E

Sight-Reading for the Contemporary Guitarist

NOTES ON EACH STRING

Examples 2.12–2.17 show the notes for each string of the guitar up to the 15th fret. Each example is shown twice, the second time using *enharmonic equivalents*—pitches that sound the same but are spelled differently, such as C♯ and D♭, or E♯ and F. (Note that while these examples combine flats and sharps by way of illustration, sharps are usually used when ascending, flats when descending.) The fact that one note can be played in many different places on the guitar is what makes sight-reading on this instrument challenging . . . but not impossible.

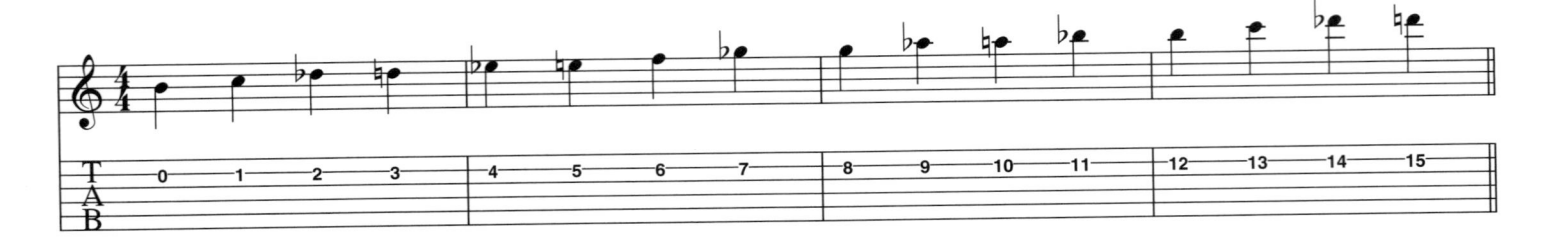

EXAMPLE 2.12: NOTES ON THE 1ST STRING

EXAMPLE 2.13: NOTES ON THE 2ND STRING

EXAMPLE 2.14: NOTES ON THE 3RD STRING

Sight-Reading for the Contemporary Guitarist 17

EXAMPLE 2.15: NOTES ON THE 4TH STRING

EXAMPLE 2.16: NOTES ON THE 5TH STRING

EXAMPLE 2.17: NOTES ON THE 6TH STRING

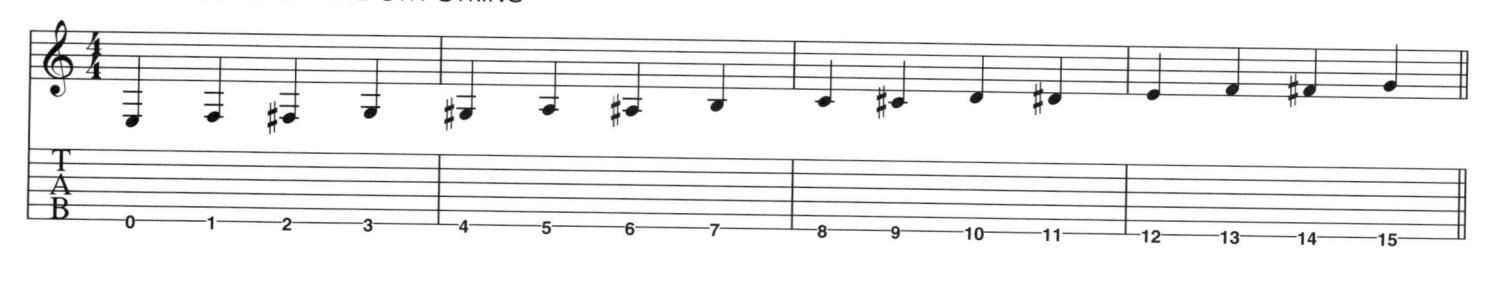

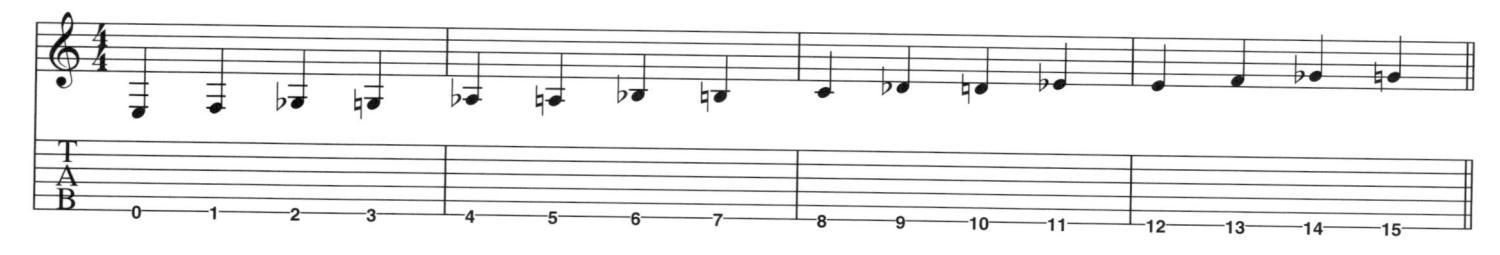

18 Sight-Reading for the Contemporary Guitarist

SINGLE-STRING READING EXERCISES

Examples 2.18–2.23 are designed to improve your knowledge of the notes on each string of the guitar. Practice them slowly at first, making sure you keep good time; this might be a good opportunity to use your metronome. The exercises are *atonal* (they don't have a key or a key signature), so you'll need to rely on your reading skills more so than your ears. Once you master an exercise, gradually increase the tempo for a greater challenge.

EXAMPLE 2.18: 1ST-STRING ETUDE

EXAMPLE 2.19: 2ND-STRING ETUDE

EXAMPLE 2.20: 3RD-STRING ETUDE

Sight-Reading for the Contemporary Guitarist   19

EXAMPLE 2.21: 4TH-STRING ETUDE

EXAMPLE 2.22: 5TH-STRING ETUDE

EXAMPLE 2.23: 6TH-STRING ETUDE

Chapter 3—Position Reading, C Major

One of the best ways to expand your sight-reading skills is to read music that we can think of as being in familiar territory. When improvising, for example, we often have favorite fingerings that we use, and we can apply the same concept to sight-reading. Since most of the music we play is in one key or another, it makes sense to try to read music using specific scale fingerings as a starting point.

OCTAVE SHAPES

There are five different *octave shapes* (octave intervals on the fretboard) on the guitar, three of which span one octave, two of which span two octaves. These shapes appear individually in the diagrams at right, and together on the fretboard below. The shapes in these examples are built on C, but because the shapes are *movable*—that is, they can be moved up or down the fretboard—you can use them on any note.

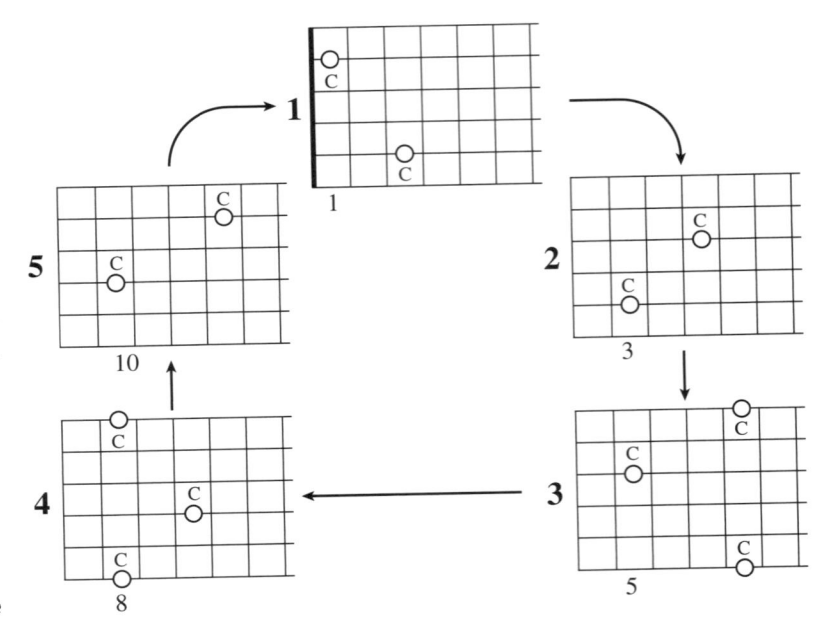

Here are all of the octave shapes together on the fretboard. Notice how they repeat after the 12 fret.

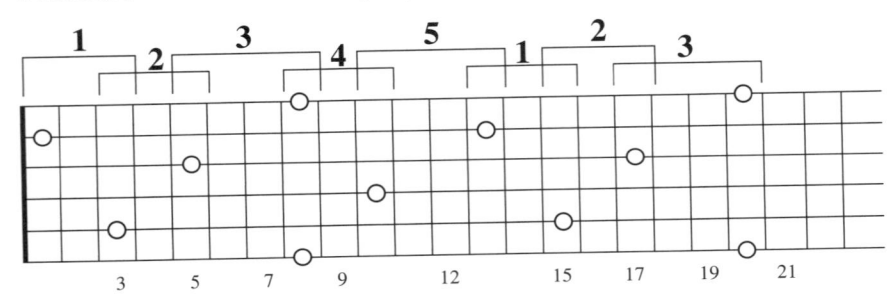

MAJOR SCALE SHAPES

The diagrams at right show the major scale shapes related to the octave shapes above. In each example, the *tonic* (the first note of the scale) corresponding to the octave shapes is shown with white dots, while the other notes of the scale are shown with black dots. These examples show a C Major scale, but again, the shapes can be moved up and down the fretboard for any major scale you choose.

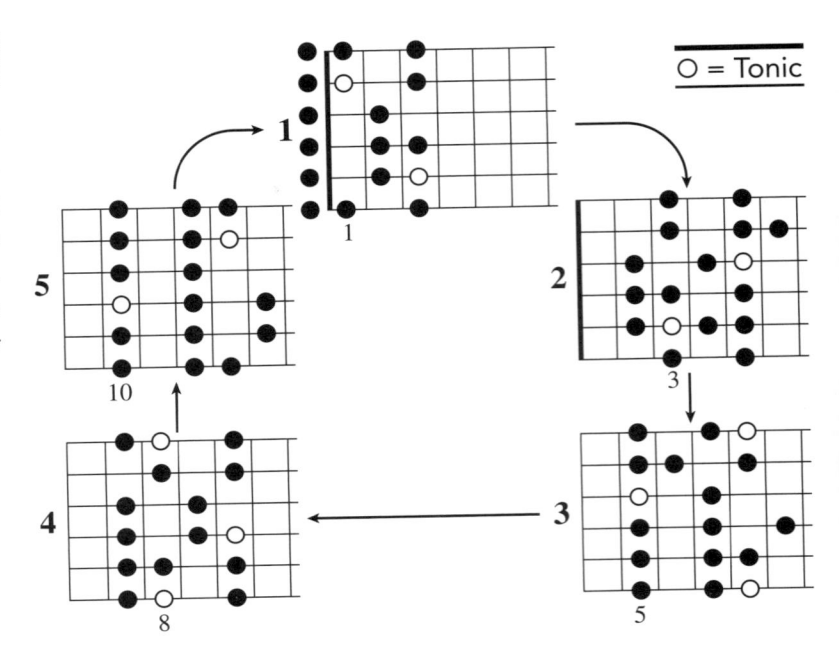

Positions on the Guitar

A *position* is a group of four frets on the fretboard, the name of which is determined by the placement of your 1st finger. For example, if your 1st finger is on the 1st fret (meaning that your 2nd, 3rd, and 4th fingers fall naturally on the 2nd, 3rd and 4th frets), you're in 1st position. Roman numerals are used to denote positions, so 1st position is shown as I (see the Roman numeral review below). If your 1st finger is on the 2nd fret, you're in 2nd position (II), and so on. The position that uses the open strings and the first four frets is called *open position*.

It is common to reach one or two frets below, or one or two frets above, the four frets of any position. For example, when in 2nd position, you may have to reach down to the 1st fret with the 1st finger or up to the 6th or 7th fret with the 4th finger; but you are still in 2nd position.

As you learn to sight-read, you'll find that some positions work just as well as others in a given situation, while in other instances, a certain position may work better than any other. Often, a single piece is most easily played by using a combination of different positions. Most of the exercises in this book will indicate which position or positions to use. As you become more comfortable and experienced with different positions, you should explore and experiment with different possibilities for positions in the same piece.

To illustrate the idea of positions, the fretboard diagram below shows the 1st, 7th and 13th positions on the guitar fretboard. The 13th fret has the same notes as the 1st fret, one octave higher. Because there are 12 half steps in an octave, and a half step is equal to one fret, notes and shapes on the fretboard repeat an octave higher every 12 frets. So, to find a note one octave up, just add 12 to the fret number. A chord shape you play in open position, for example, will sound exactly one octave higher in 12th position (replace the open strings with fretted notes on the 12th fret); a chord shape in 1st position will sound an octave higher in 13th position; a chord you play in 2nd position will sound an octave higher in 14th position; and so on.

On most electric guitars, the 20th position is the highest possible position (the 24th fret is the highest fret). Acoustic and classical guitars have considerably fewer frets.

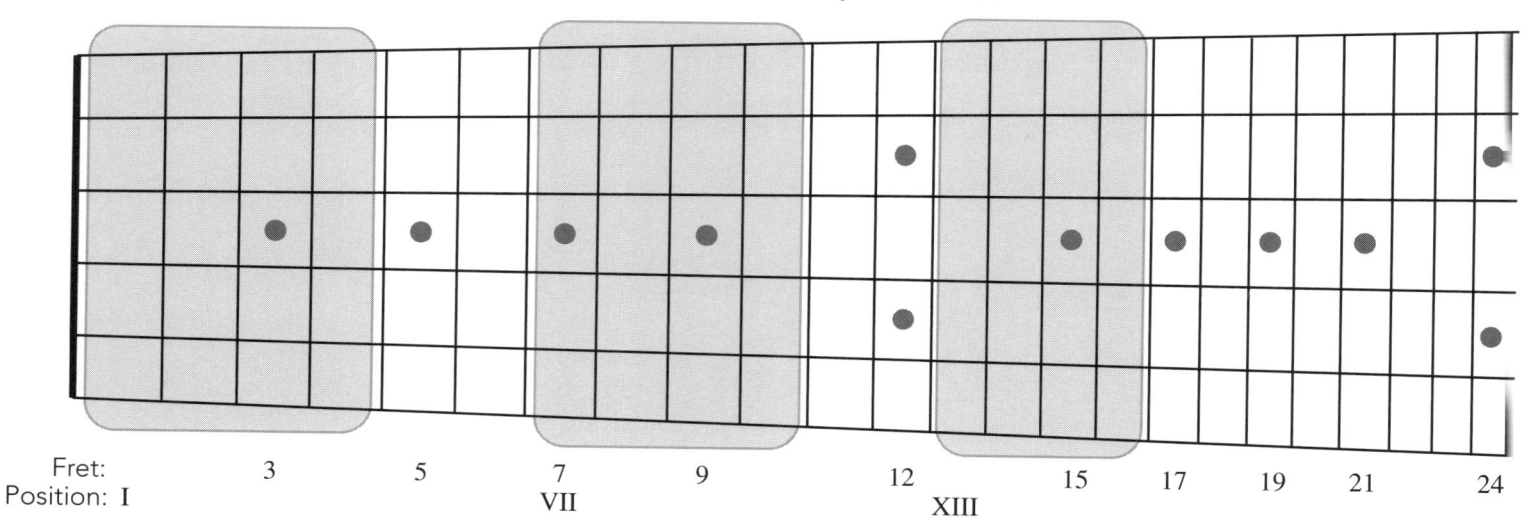

Fret: 3   5   7   9   12   15   17   19   21   24
Position: I   VII   XIII

I......1	IV......4	VII......7	X......10	XIII......13	XVI......16
II......2	V......5	VIII......8	XI......11	XIV......14	XVII......17
III......3	VI......6	IX......9	XII......12	XV......15	XVIII......18

C Major Scale Positions

The fretboard diagrams below show the positions for the C Major scale based on the shapes you learned on page 20. The key of C Major has no sharps or flats.

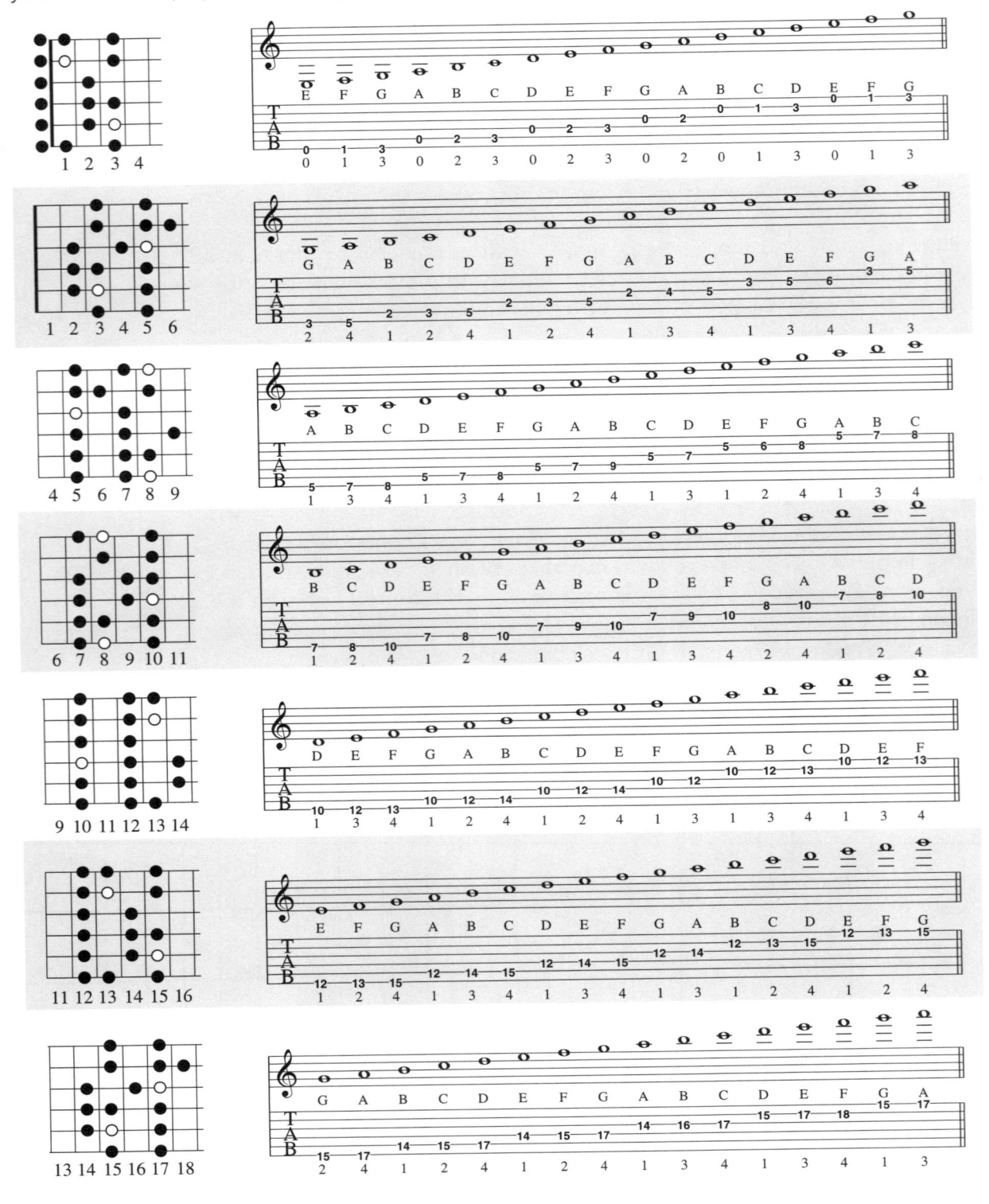

C Major Exercises

Examples 3.1–3.6 are in C Major. Each example includes the different possible playing positions. Try playing each example in each of the given positions, referring to the fretboard diagrams on page 22 if you need a reminder. As you begin to practice sight-reading, it's good to remember that briefly previewing the music before you begin to play can be very helpful. Looking at the music ahead of time will help you identify potential problem areas, and it will also help you discover features that can make sight-reading earlier—sections that repeat, repetitive phrases, and so on. As you become more proficient as a sight-reader, it's good to get in the habit of looking ahead as you play, which will allow you to anticipate and prepare for what comes next.

Example 3.1
Play in open, 2nd, 5th and 7th positions.

Example 3.2
Play in open and 2nd positions.

24 Sight-Reading for the Contemporary Guitarist

EXAMPLE 3.3
Play in 5th, 7th and 10th positions.

EXAMPLE 3.4
Play in 7th, 10th and 12th positions.

Sight-Reading for the Contemporary Guitarist 25

EXAMPLE 3.5

Play in 12th and 14th positions. Remember that 14th position uses the same shape as 2nd position.

EXAMPLE 3.6

Play in 12th and 14th positions.

Reading Intervals and Triads

Be sure that you're thoroughly familiar with the fingerboard chart pages 14–15 before continuing.

Reading Intervals

One of the most common ways to harmonize a melody on the guitar is with *harmonic intervals*, otherwise known as *dyads* or *double stops* (two notes played simultaneously by a single player). The first requirement for being able to sight-read harmonic intervals is fully understanding them. Refer to pages 25–28 of *Theory for the Contemporary Guitarist* and pages 11–18 of *Ear Training for the Contemporary Guitarist* to become fully acquainted with intervals.

The next important step is to become familiar with the appearance of each interval. The example below gives several examples of each *simple interval* (intervals smaller than and including the octave). *Compound intervals* (those wider than an octave) are far less idiomatic to the guitar, and we seldom have to read them, except in the classical literature.

It is important to make the following observations:

- Both notes in an odd-numbered simple interval—a unison (1), 3rd, 5th and 7th—occur on spaces or lines. For example, in a 3rd, if the bottom note is on a space, the upper one will be on the next higher space. If the bottom note is on a line, the upper one will be on the next higher line.

- The notes in an even-numbered simple interval—a 2nd, 4th, 6th or octave (8)—will be on lines *and* spaces. For example, if the bottom note of a 4th is on a space, the upper note will be on a line, and vice versa.

- The smaller the interval number, the closer the notes are on the staff.

Study the appearances of these intervals on the staff and their most common shapes, which can be moved up and down the fretboard. Notice that interval shapes on the fretboard are different when they involve the 2nd string, because of the interval of a 3rd between the 3rd and 2nd strings in standard guitar tuning.

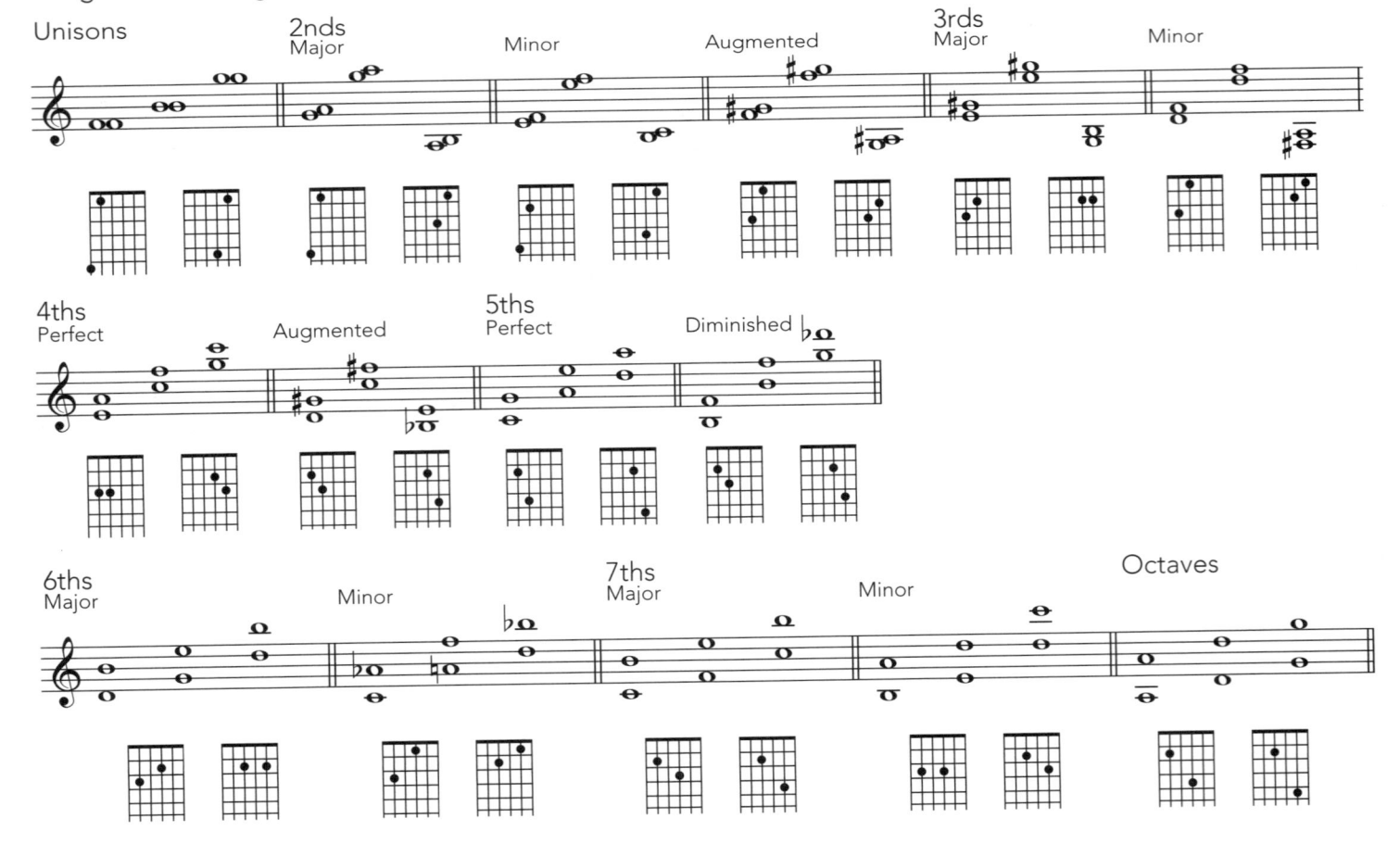

TRIADS

The first requirement for reading triads is the same as for reading intervals: You must completely understand them. (For a review of triads and inversions, refer to pages 29–36 of *Theory for the Contemporary Guitarist* and pages 20–30 of *Ear Training for the Contemporary Guitarist*, both published by the National Guitar Workshop/Alfred Publishing.)

Below are some triads and their inversions, so that you can familiarize yourself with how they look on the staff and their common shapes on the fretboard. Here are some important observations:

- Root position triads have all of the notes on spaces or on lines. If the root is on a space, the 3rd and 5th will be also.

- 1st inversion triads have a 3rd between the bottom two notes, and a 4th between the top two.

- 2nd inversion triads have a 4th between the bottom two notes, and a 3rd between the top two.

Study these carefully. Notice that triad shapes on the fretboard are different when they involve the 2nd string, becuase of the interval of a 3rd between the 3rd and 2nd strings in standard guitar tuning.

Root Position

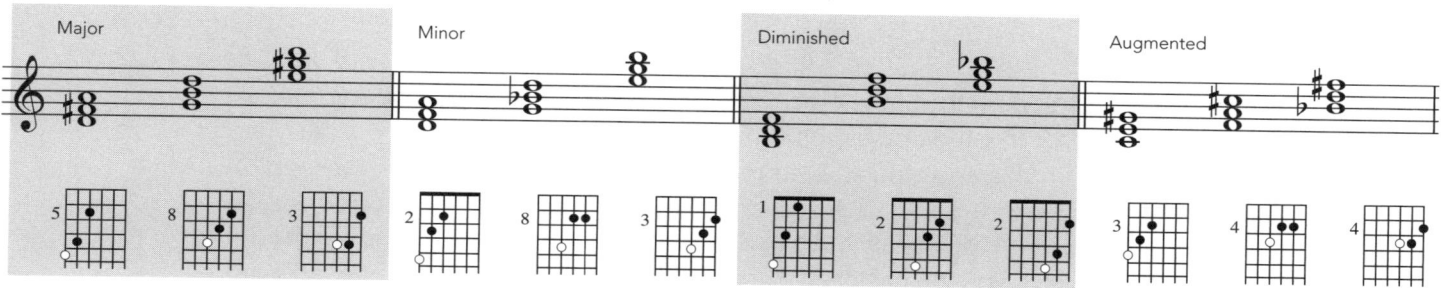

1st Inversion

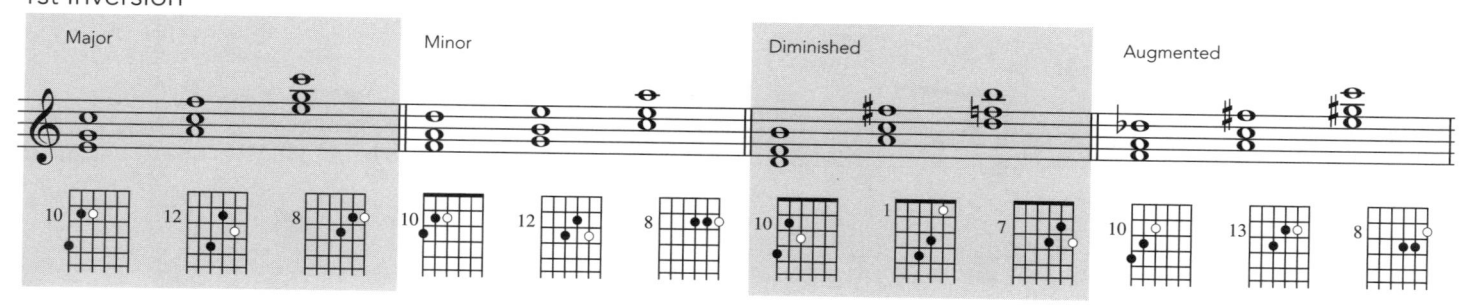

2nd Inversion

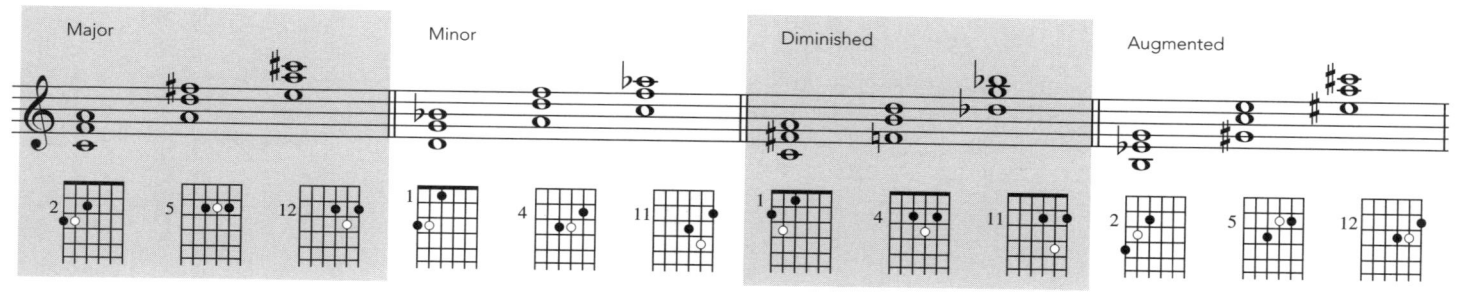

C Major Harmonic Reading Exercises

Examples 3.7–3.9 are harmonic reading exercises—that is, they use harmonic intervals and chords.

Example 3.7
Play in both the 12th and 14th positions.

Example 3.8
Play in 12th position.

Example 3.9
Example 3.9 uses multiple positions in the same piece. In some cases, changing positions makes certain passages easier to play; in other cases, changing positions is absolutely necessary in order to reach certain notes. In this and similar examples throughout the book, three possible combinations of positions (labeled A, B and C) are given. In most cases, even more options are possible. Familiarizing yourself with the possibilities of different positions is essential in sharpening your sight-reading skills. Once you've mastered the given combinations, try combining them (for example, using parts of A and parts of B), and use the fretboard knowledge you've gained so far to explore even more possibilities. Pay particular attention to how different positions affect the sound of the music and the feel of your playing.

Chapter 4–G Major Reading Exercises

G MAJOR SCALE POSITIONS

The fretboard diagrams below show the positions for the G Major scale. Notice that one of the roots is an open string in open position. The key of G Major has one sharp (F#).

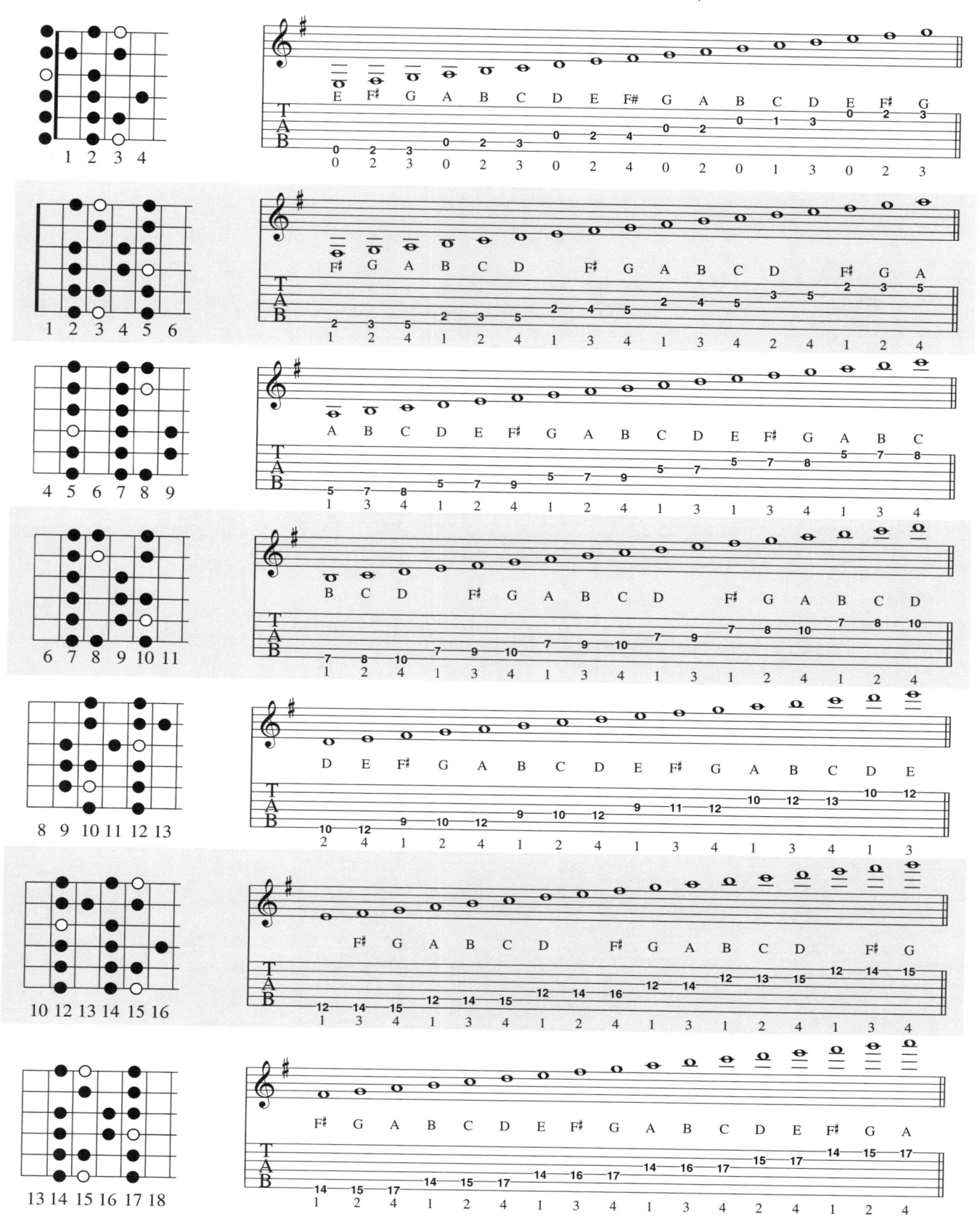

G Major Exercises

Example 4.1
Play in open and 2nd positions.

Example 4.2
Play in open and 2nd positions.

Example 4.3
Play in 5th, 7th and 9th positions.

Sight-Reading for the Contemporary Guitarist 31

EXAMPLE 4.4

Play in 5th, 7th, 9th and 12th positions.

EXAMPLE 4.5

Play in 7th, 9th, 12th and 14th positions.

EXAMPLE 4.6

Play in 9th, 12th and 14th positions.

Example 4.7
Play in 12th and 14th positions.

Example 4.8
Play in 14th position.

Example 4.9
Play in 14th position.

Sight-Reading for the Contemporary Guitarist   33

G MAJOR HARMONIC READING EXERCISES

Examples 4.10–4.12 are in G Major.

EXAMPLE 4.10

Play in open, 2nd, 5th and 7th positions.

EXAMPLE 4.11

Play in open, 2nd, 5th and 7th positions.

EXAMPLE 4.12

Chapter 5—F Major Reading Exercises

F Major Scale Positions

The fretboard diagrams below show the positions for the F Major scale based on the shapes you learned on page 20. The key of F Major has one flat (B♭).

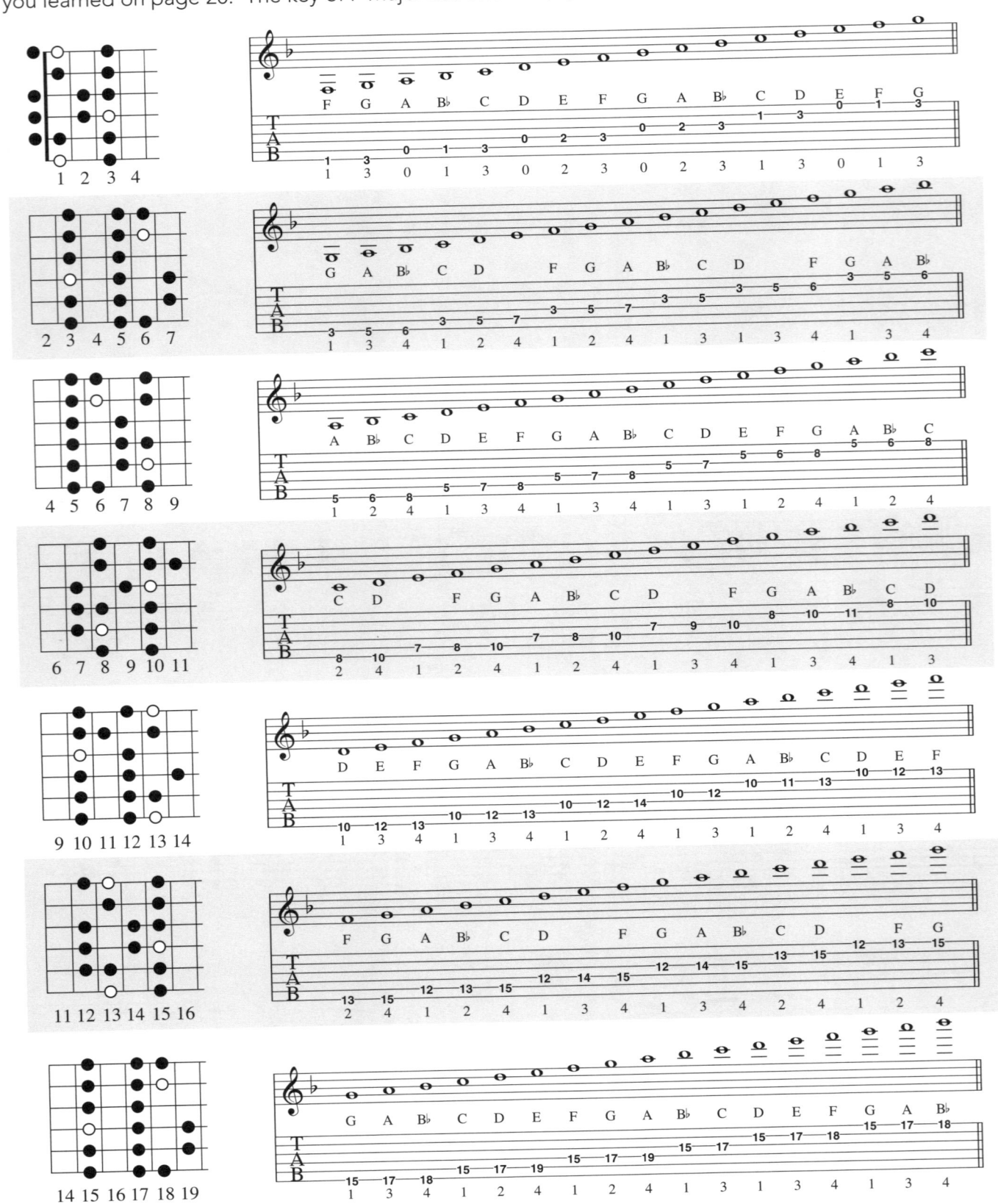

F Major Exercises

Example 5.1
Play in open position.

36 Sight-Reading for the Contemporary Guitarist

Example 5.4
Play in 5th and 7th positions.

Example 5.5
Play in 3rd, 5th, 7th, 10th and 12th positions.

Example 5.6
Play in 10th, 12th and 15th positions.

Sight-Reading for the Contemporary Guitarist

Example 5.7
Play in 10th, 12th and 15th positions.

Example 5.8
Play in 12th and 15th positions.

Example 5.9
Play in 12th and 15th positions.

F Major Harmonic Reading Exercises

Examples 5.10–5.12 are in F Major. Remember, while playing in any position, you may have to move below it or above it briefly. This does not change the fact that you are essentially playing in that position.

These harmonic exercises are best handled without an eye to staying in any one position. You will need to move freely along the strings to finger the intervals and chords.

Example 5.10
Play in open, 3rd, 5th and 7th positions.

Example 5.11
Play in 3rd, 5th and 7th positions.

Example 5.12

Chapter 6–D Major Reading Exercises

D Major Scale Positions

The fretboard diagrams below show the positions for the D Major scale based on the shapes you learned on page 14. Notice that one of the roots is an open string in open and 12th positions. The key of D Major has two sharps (F# and C#).

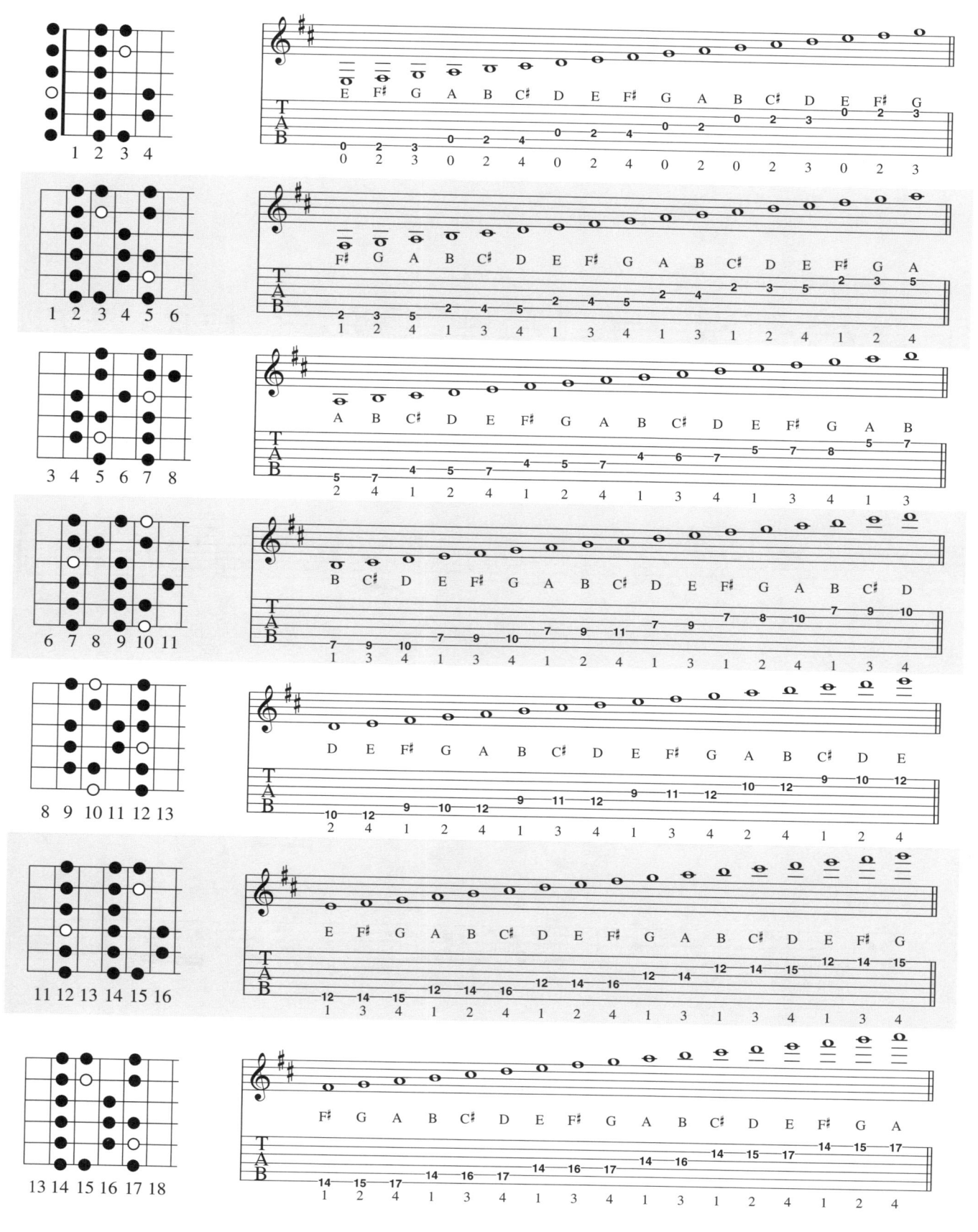

D Major Exercises

Example 6.1
Play in open, 2nd and 4th positions.

Example 6.2
Play in open, 2nd and 4th positions.

Example 6.3
Play in open, 2nd, 4th, 7th and 9th positions.

Sight-Reading for the Contemporary Guitarist

Example 6.4
Play in 4th, 7th, 9th, 12th and 14th positions.

Example 6.5
Play in 4th, 7th, 12th and 14th positions.

Example 6.6
Play in 4th, 7th, 9th, 12th and 14th positions.

42 Sight-Reading for the Contemporary Guitarist

Example 6.7
Play in 12th and 14th positions.

Example 6.8
Play in 12th and 14th positions.

Example 6.9
Play in 14th position.

D Major Harmonic Reading Exercises

Examples 6.10–6.12 are in D Major.

Example 6.10

Play in 5th, 7th and 9th positions.

Example 6.11

Play in 5th, 7th, 9th, 12th, 14th and 17th positions.

Example 6.12

Play in 5th position. Notice that you'll need to stretch to play the high D in measure 3.

Chapter 7—B♭ Major Reading Exercises

B♭ MAJOR SCALE POSITIONS

The fretboard diagrams below show the positions for the B♭ Major scale based on the shapes you learned on page 20. The key of B♭ Major has two flats (B♭ and E♭). By now, you're probably starting to see the connections among the scale positions for the different keys. Try comparing the B♭ Major positions to the ones you've already learned, noting similarities among the shapes.

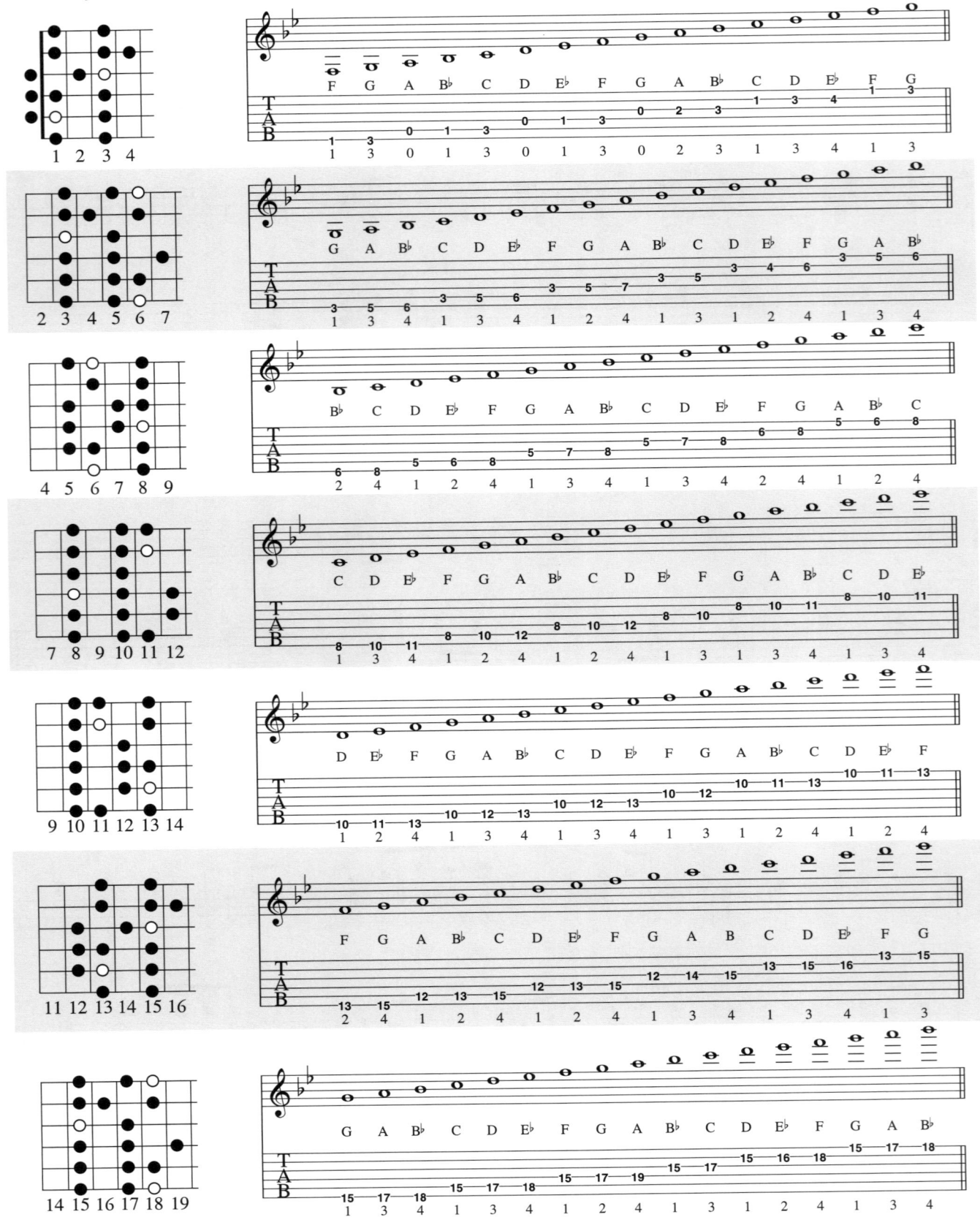

B♭ Major Exercises

Example 7.1

Play in open position.

Example 7.2

Play in open position.

Example 7.3

Play in 3rd and 5th positions.

46 Sight-Reading for the Contemporary Guitarist

Example 7.4
Play in 5th position.

Example 7.5
Play in 5th, 8th, 10th, 12th and 15th positions.

Example 7.6
Play in 5th, 8th, 10th and 12th positions.

Sight-Reading for the Contemporary Guitarist 47

Example 7.7
Play in 10th, 12th and 15th positions.

Example 7.8
Play in 10th, 12th and 15th positions.

Example 7.9
Play in 15th position.

B♭ Major Harmonic Reading Exercises

Examples 7.10–7.12 are in B♭ Major.

Example 7.10

Play in 5th, 8th and 10th positions.

Example 7.11

Play in 5th and 8th positions.

Example 7.12

Chapter 8—A Major Reading Exercises

A Major Scale Positions

The fretboard diagrams below show the positions for the A Major scale based on the shapes you learned on page 20. Notice that one of the roots is an open string in open position. The key of A Major has three sharps (F#, C# and G#).

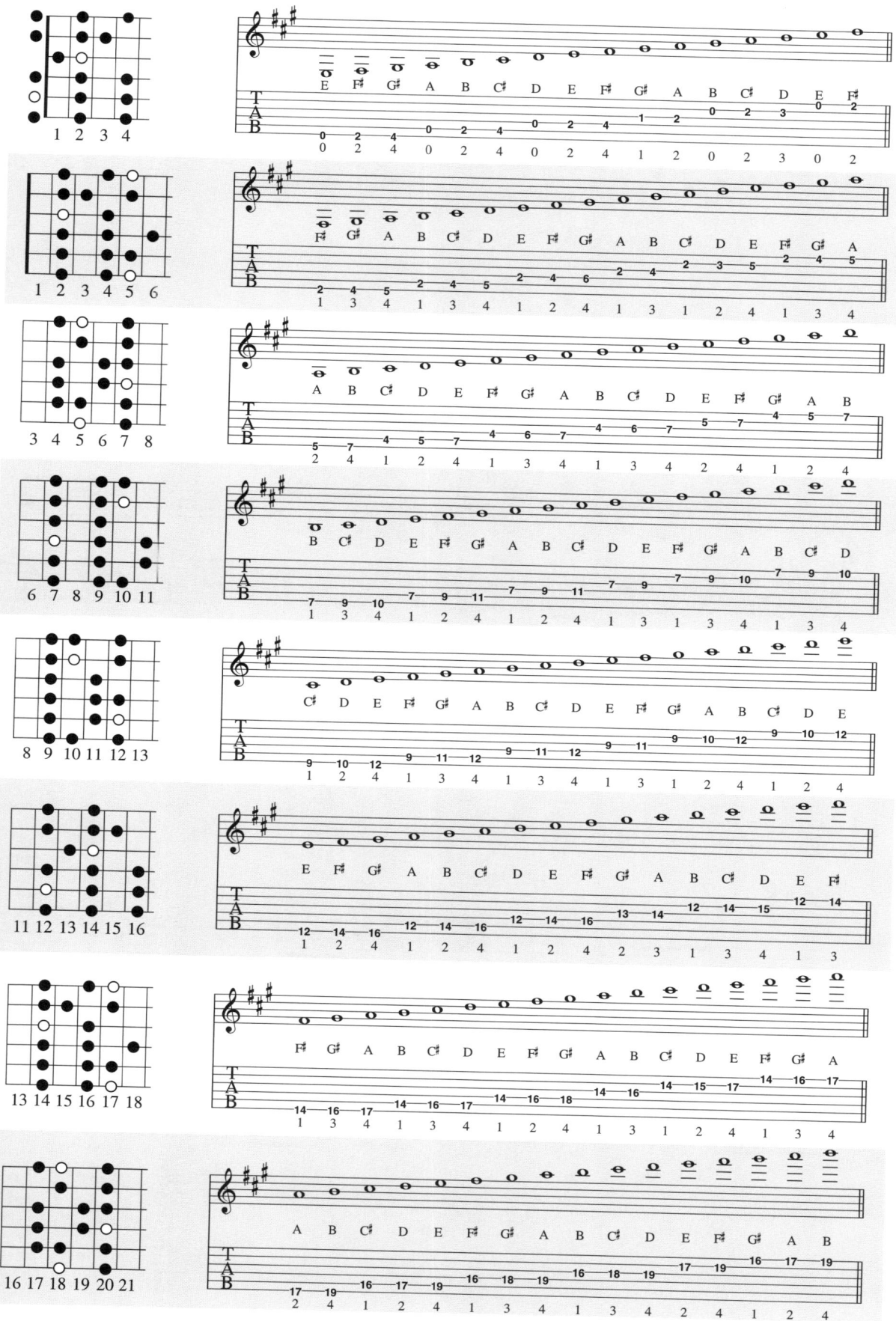

A Major Exercises

Example 8.1
Play in open position.

Example 8.2
Play in open and 2nd positions.

Example 8.3
Play in open and 2nd positions.

EXAMPLE 8.4
Play in 4th and 7th positions.

EXAMPLE 8.5
Play in 4th, 7th, 9th, 12th and 14th positions.

EXAMPLE 8.6
Play in 7th, 9th, 12th and 14th positions.

EXAMPLE 8.7
Play in 9th, 12th and 14th positions.

EXAMPLE 8.8
Play in 9th, 12th and 14th positions.

EXAMPLE 8.9
Play in 14th position.

Sight-Reading for the Contemporary Guitarist 53

A Major Harmonic Reading Exercises

Examples 8.10–8.12 are in A Major.

Example 8.10

Play in 4th, 7th and 9th positions.

Example 8.11

Play in 4th, 7th and 9th positions.

Example 8.12

Chapter 9–E♭ Major Reading Exercises

E♭ Major Scale Fingerings

The fretboard diagrams below show the positions for the E♭ Major scale based on the shapes you learned on page 20. The key of E♭ Major has three flats (B♭, E♭ and A♭).

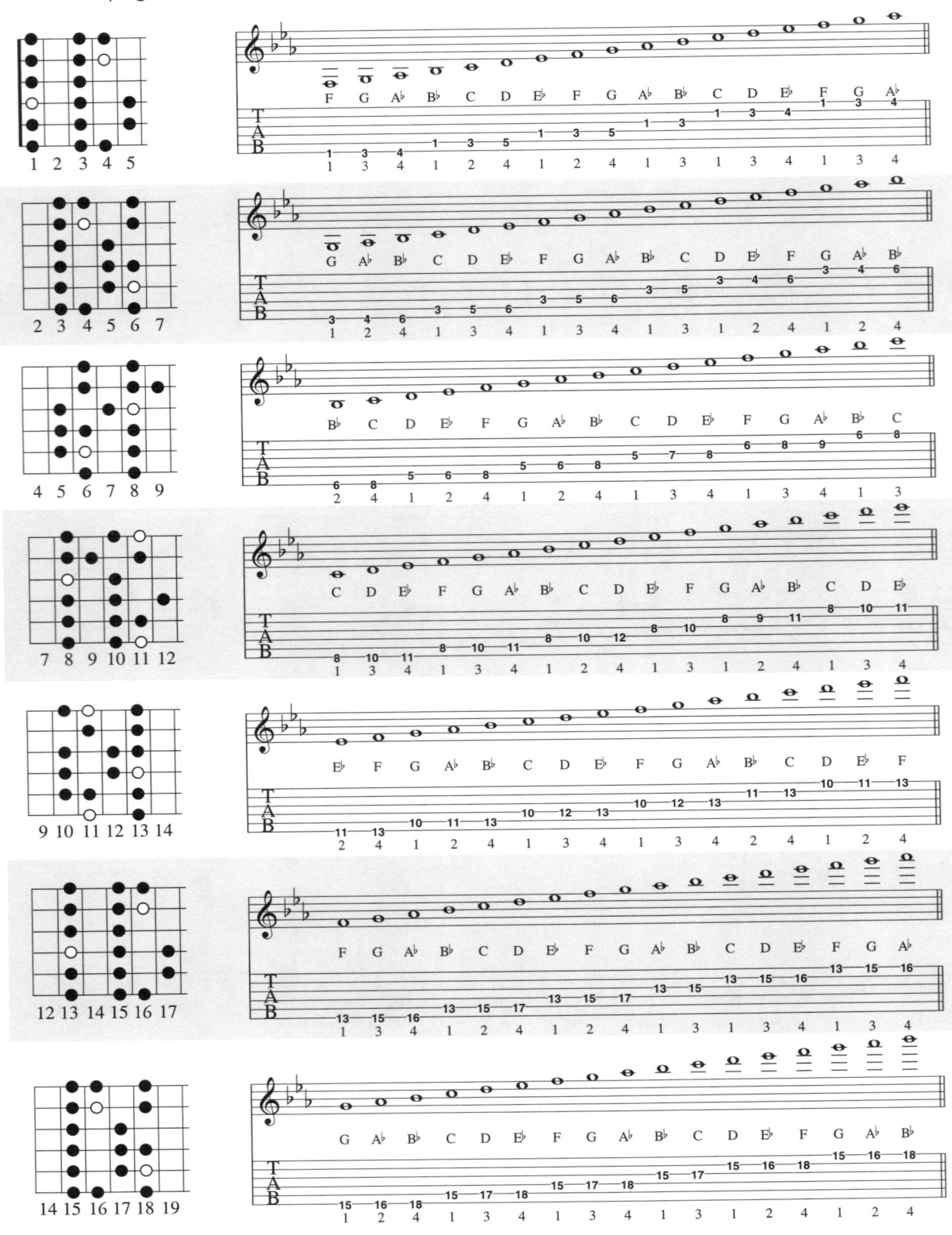

E♭ Major Exercises

Example 9.1

Play in 1st and 3rd positions.

Example 9.2

Play in 3rd and 5th positions.

Example 9.3

Play in 3rd, 5th, 8th and 13th positions.

56 Sight-Reading for the Contemporary Guitarist

EXAMPLE 9.4
Play in 5th position.

EXAMPLE 9.5
Play in 5th, 8th and 10th positions.

EXAMPLE 9.6
Play in 3rd, 5th, 8th, 10th, 12th and 15th positions.

Sight-Reading for the Contemporary Guitarist

EXAMPLE 9.7
Play in 13th and 15th positions.

EXAMPLE 9.8
Play in 15th position.

EXAMPLE 9.9
Play in 15th position.

E♭ Major Harmonic Reading Exercises

Examples 9.10–9.12 are in E♭ Major.

Example 9.10
Play in 3rd and 5th positions.

Example 9.11

Example 9.12

Chapter 10—E Major Reading Exercises

E MAJOR SCALE POSITIONS

We've finally made it to a "real" guitar key! The fretboard diagrams below show the positions for the E Major scale based on the shapes you learned on page 20. Notice that two of the roots are open strings in open position. The key of E Major has four sharps (F#, C#, G# and D#).

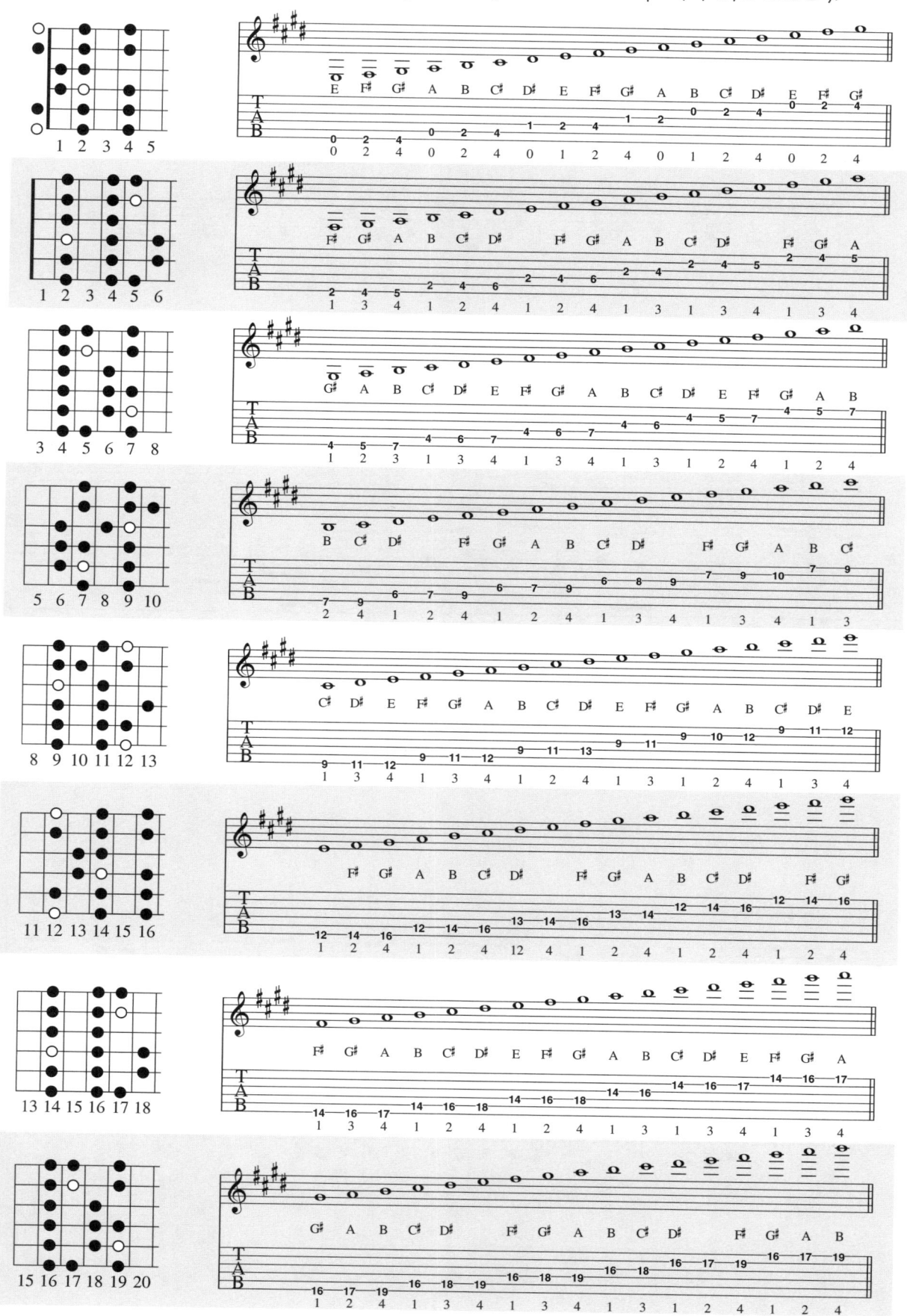

E Major Exercises

Example 10.1

Play in open position.

Example 10.2

Play in open position.

Example 10.3

Play in open, 2nd and 4th positions.

Sight-Reading for the Contemporary Guitarist

Example 10.4
Play in 4th and 6th positions.

Example 10.5
Play in 9th and 12th positions.

Example 10.6
Play in 9th and 12th positions.

62 Sight-Reading for the Contemporary Guitarist

Example 10.7

Play in 12th and 14th positions.

Example 10.8

Play in 12th and 14th positions.

Example 10.9

Play in 14th position.

E Major Harmonic Reading Exercises

Examples 10.10–10.12 are in E Major.

Example 10.10

Example 10.11

Play in 11th position.

Example 10.12

Chapter 11 – A♭ Major Reading Exercises

A♭ Major Scale Positions

The fretboard diagrams below show the positions for the A♭ Major scale based on the shapes you learned on page 20. The key of A♭ Major has four flats (B♭, E♭, A♭ and D♭). Are you beginning to commit the scale positions to memory? Once you've looked at these, practice playing each scale until you can play it without referring to the diagrams. Then, go back and do the same for the scale positions we've already looked at.

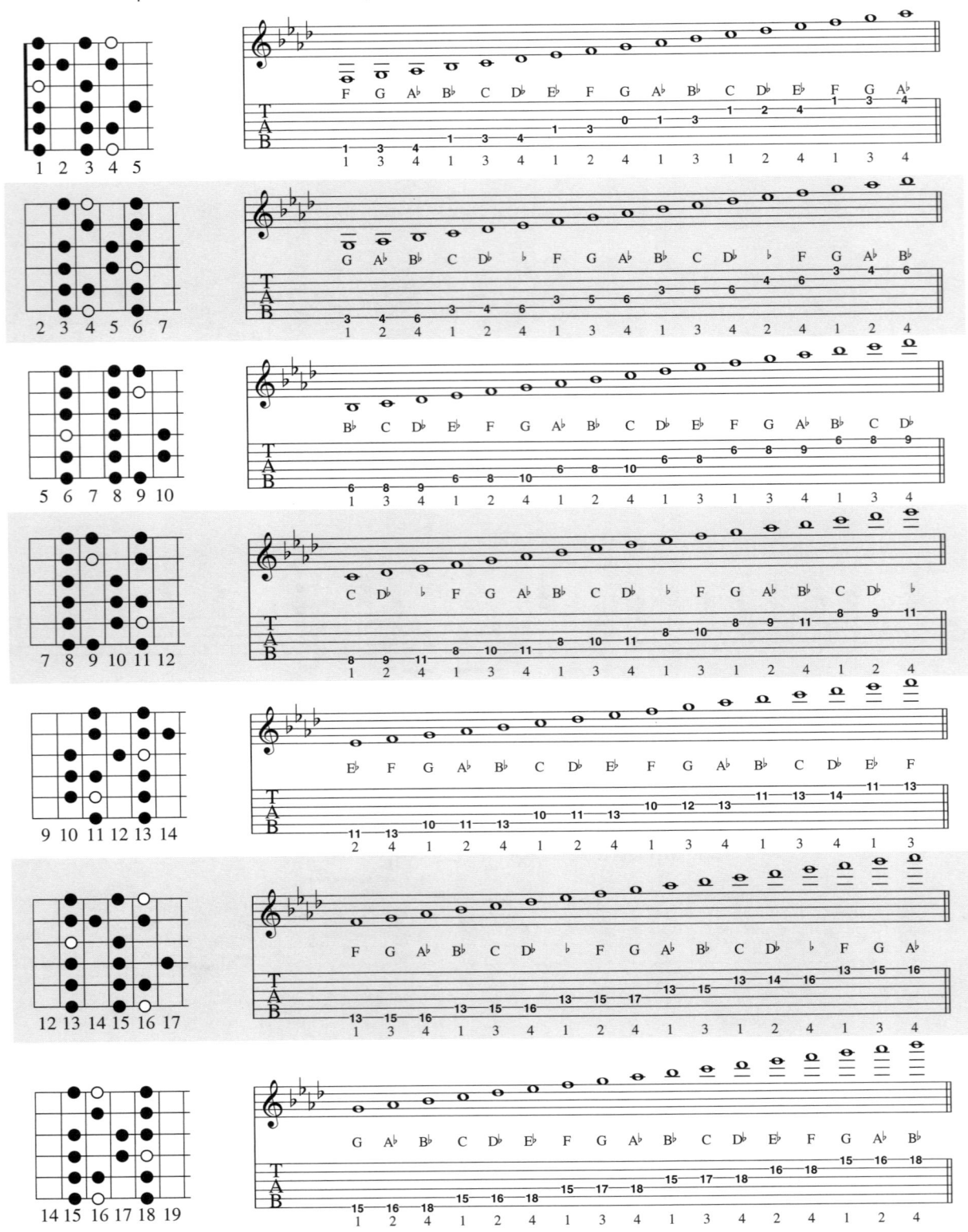

A♭ Major Exercises

Example 11.1

Play in 1st position.

Example 11.2

Play in 1st and 3rd positions.

Example 11.3

Play in 3rd position.

Example 11.4

Play in 6th, 8th and 10th positions.

Example 11.5

Play in 8th, 10th, 13th and 15th positions.

Example 11.6

Play in 8th, 10th, 13th and 15th positions.

Sight-Reading for the Contemporary Guitarist

EXAMPLE 11.7

Play in 10th, 13th and 15th positions.

EXAMPLE 11.8

Play in 10th, 13th and 15th positions.

EXAMPLE 11.9

Play in 15th position.

A♭ Major Harmonic Reading Exercises

You know the drill by now. Examples 11.10 and 11.11 are in A♭ Major.

Example 11.10

Example 11.11

Chapter 12—B Major Reading Exercises

B MAJOR SCALE FINGERINGS

The fretboard diagrams below show the positions for the B Major scale based on the shapes you learned on page 20. The key of B Major has five sharps (F#, C# G#, D# and A#).

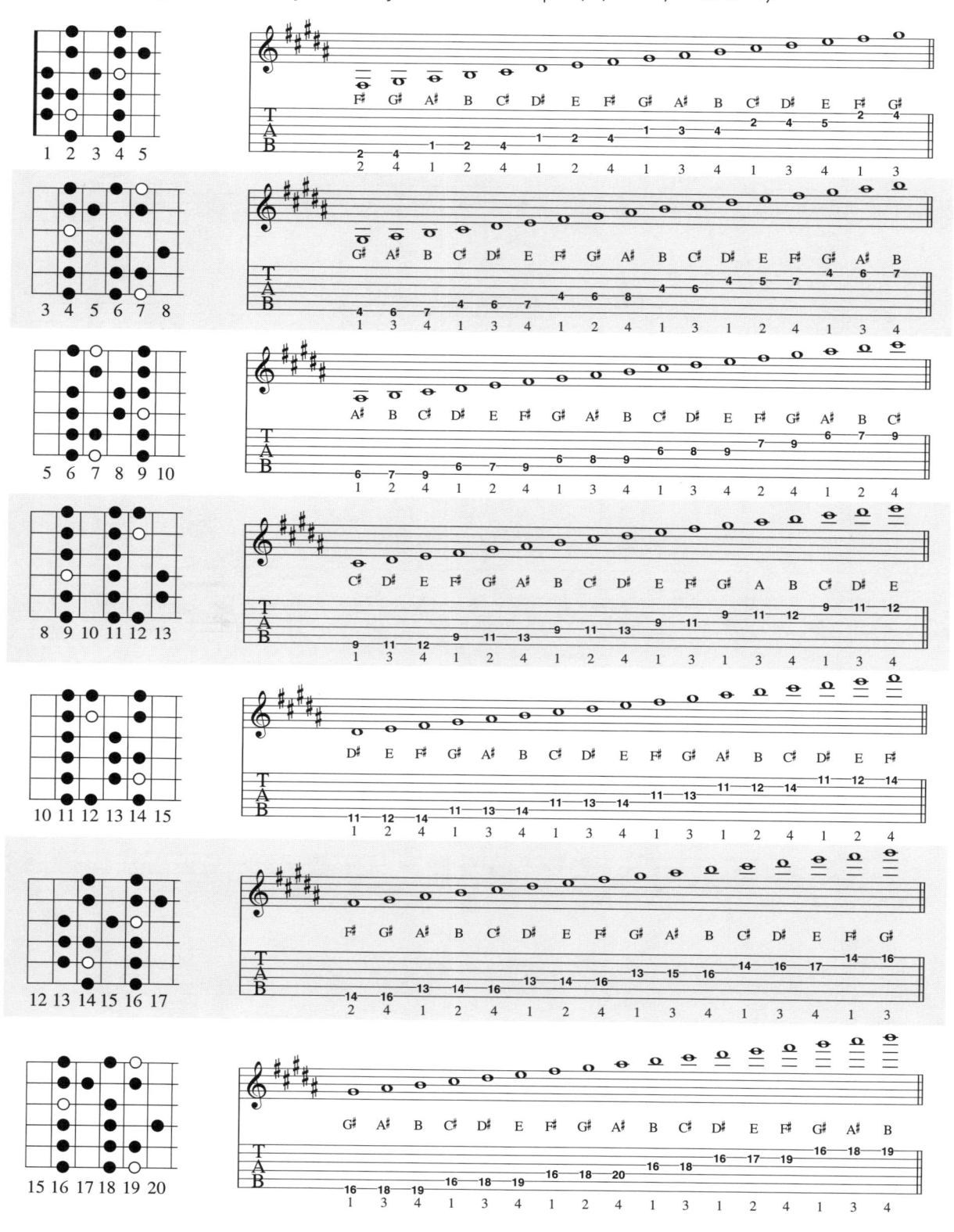

B Major Exercises

Example 12.1

Play in 1st position.

Example 12.2

Play in 1st position.

Example 12.3

Play in 4th and 6th positions.

Sight-Reading for the Contemporary Guitarist

EXAMPLE 12.4
Play in 4th and 6th positions.

EXAMPLE 12.5
Play in 6th position.

EXAMPLE 12.6
Play in 9th position.

Example 12.7
Play in 9th, 13th and 16th positions.

Example 12.8
Play in 9th, 13th and 16th positions.

Example 12.9
Play in 16th position.

Sight-Reading for the Contemporary Guitarist 73

B Major Harmonic Reading Exercises

Examples 12.10–12.12 are in B Major.

Example 12.10

Play in 1st, 4th, 7th, 9th and 11th positions.

Example 12.11

Play in 11th position.

Example 12.12

# Chapter 13—D♭ Major Reading Exercises

D♭ MAJOR SCALE POSITIONS

The fretboard diagrams below show the positions for the D♭ Major scale based on the shapes you learned on page 20. The key of D♭ major has five flats (B♭, E♭, A♭, D♭ and G♭). Are you starting to see these patterns in your sleep yet?

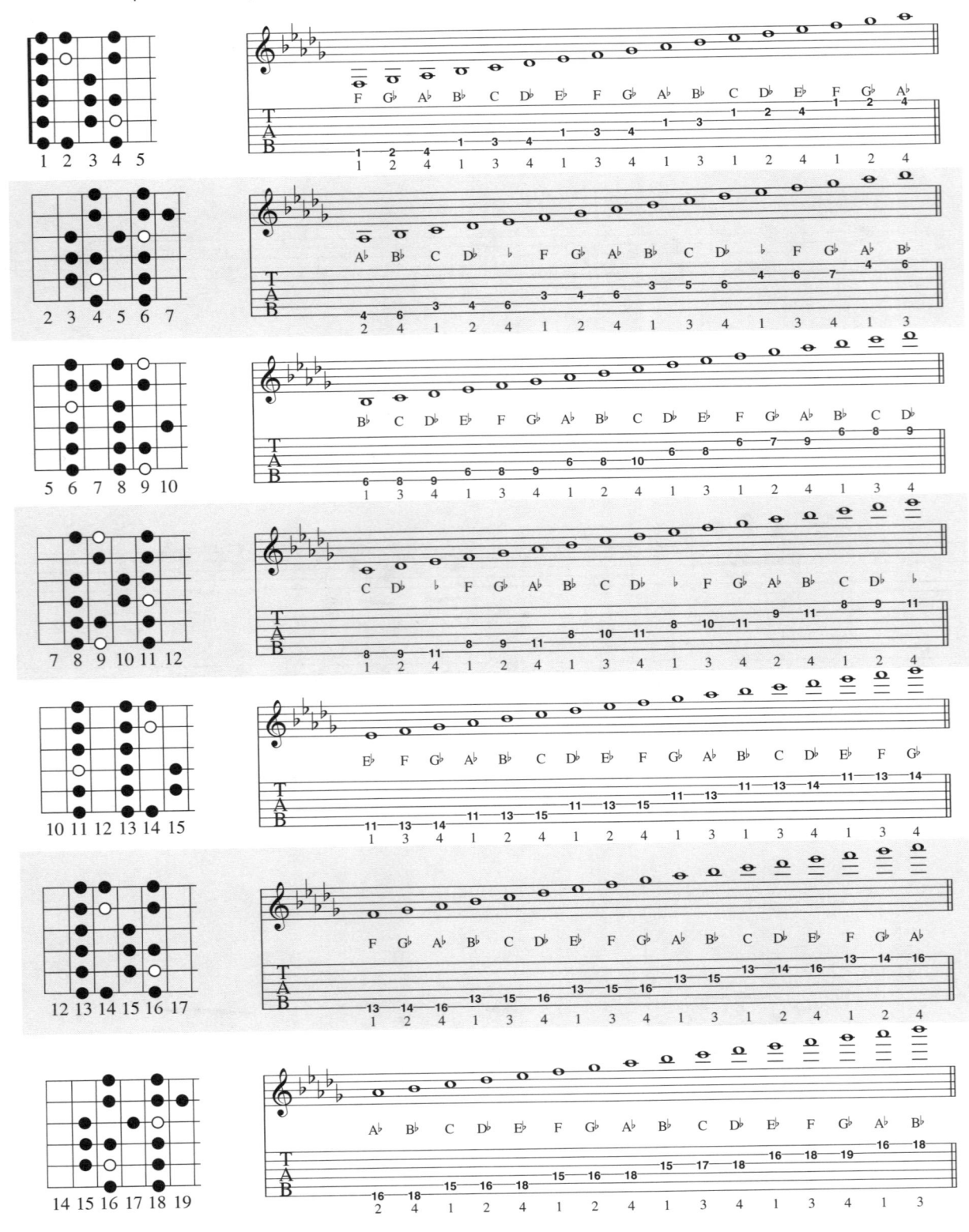

D♭ Major Exercises

Example 13.1

Play in 1st position.

Example 13.2

Play in 1st and 3rd positions.

Example 13.3

Play in 6th and 8th positions.

76 Sight-Reading for the Contemporary Guitarist

Example 13.4
Play in 6th and 8th positions.

Example 13.5
Play in 8th, 11th, 13th and 15th positions.

Example 13.6
Play in 8th, 11th, 13th and 15th positions.

Sight-Reading for the Contemporary Guitarist

EXAMPLE 13.7
Play in 11th, 13th and 15th positions.

EXAMPLE 13.8
Play in 13th and 15th positions.

EXAMPLE 13.9
Play in 13th and 15th positions.

D♭ Major Harmonic Reading Exercises

Examples 13.10–13.12 are in D♭ Major.

Example 13.10
Play in 3rd, 6th and 8th positions.

Example 13.11
Play in 1st, 3rd and 6th positions.

Example 13.12

Chapter 14 – F# Major Reading Exercises

F# Major Scale Positions

The fretboard diagrams below show the positions for the F# Major scale based on the shapes you learned on page 20. The key of F# major has six sharps (F#, C#, G#, D#, A# and E#). As you become increasingly comfortable with the scale shapes, try to stay focused on reading the music itself.

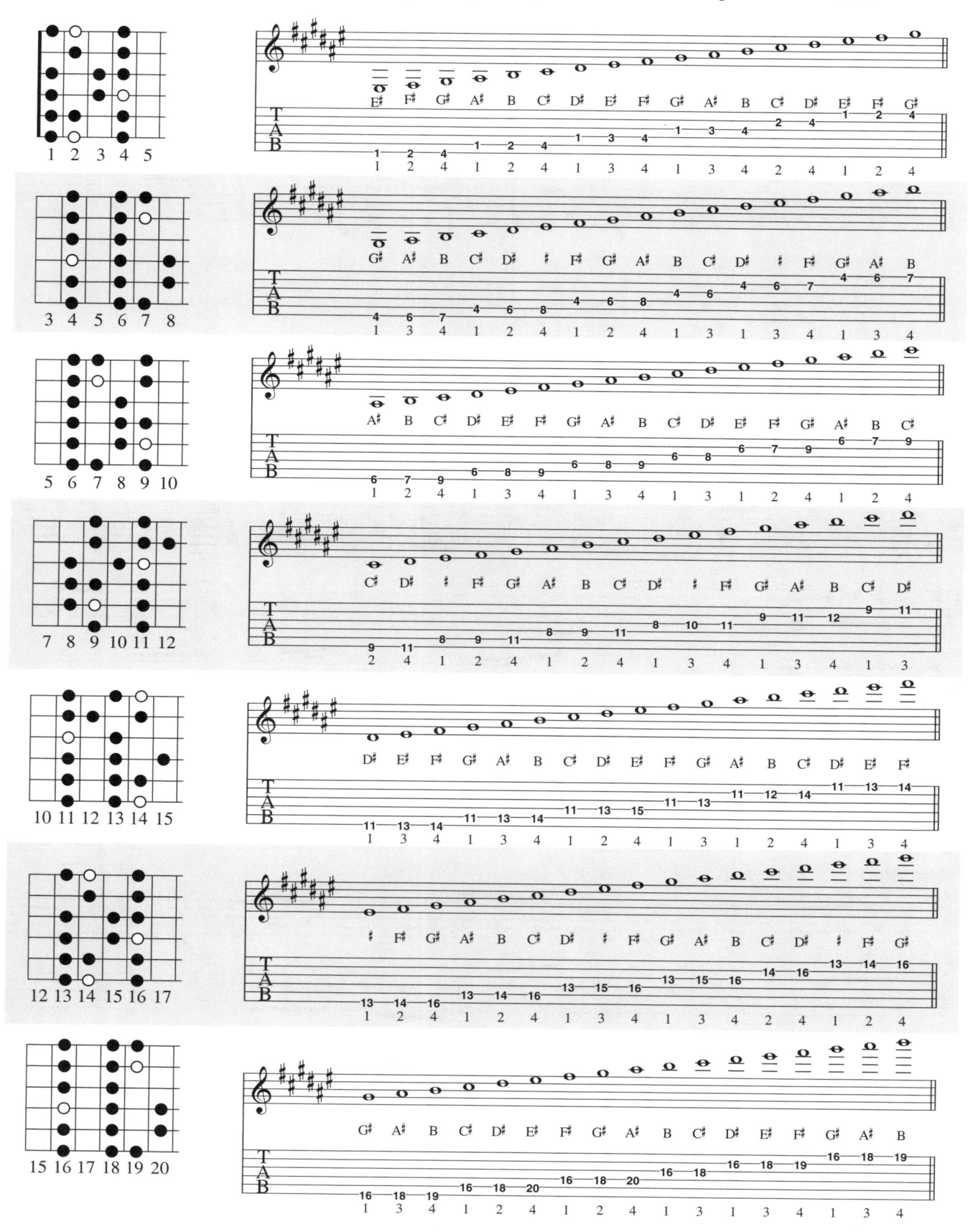

F# Major Exercises

Example 14.1
Play in 1st position.

Example 14.2
Play in 1st and 4th positions.

Example 14.3
Play in 4th position.

Sight-Reading for the Contemporary Guitarist

EXAMPLE 14.4
Play in 6th position.

EXAMPLE 14.5
Play in 6th and 8th positions.

EXAMPLE 14.6
Play in 11th and 13th positions.

Example 14.7
Play in 11th, 13th and 16th positions.

Example 14.8
Play in 13th and 16th positions.

Example 14.9
Play in 16th position.

F# Major Harmonic Reading Exercises

Examples 14.10–14.12 are in F# Major.

Example 14.10
Play in 6th position.

Example 14.11
Play in 13th position.

Example 14.12

Chapter 15 – G♭ Major Reading Exercises

G♭ Major Scale Positions

The fretboard diagrams below show the positions for the G♭ Major scale based on the shapes you learned on page 20. The key of G♭ Major has six flats (B♭, E♭, A♭, D♭, G♭ and C♭). Be sure to stay focused on reading the notes as you continue to expand your knowledge of scale positions.

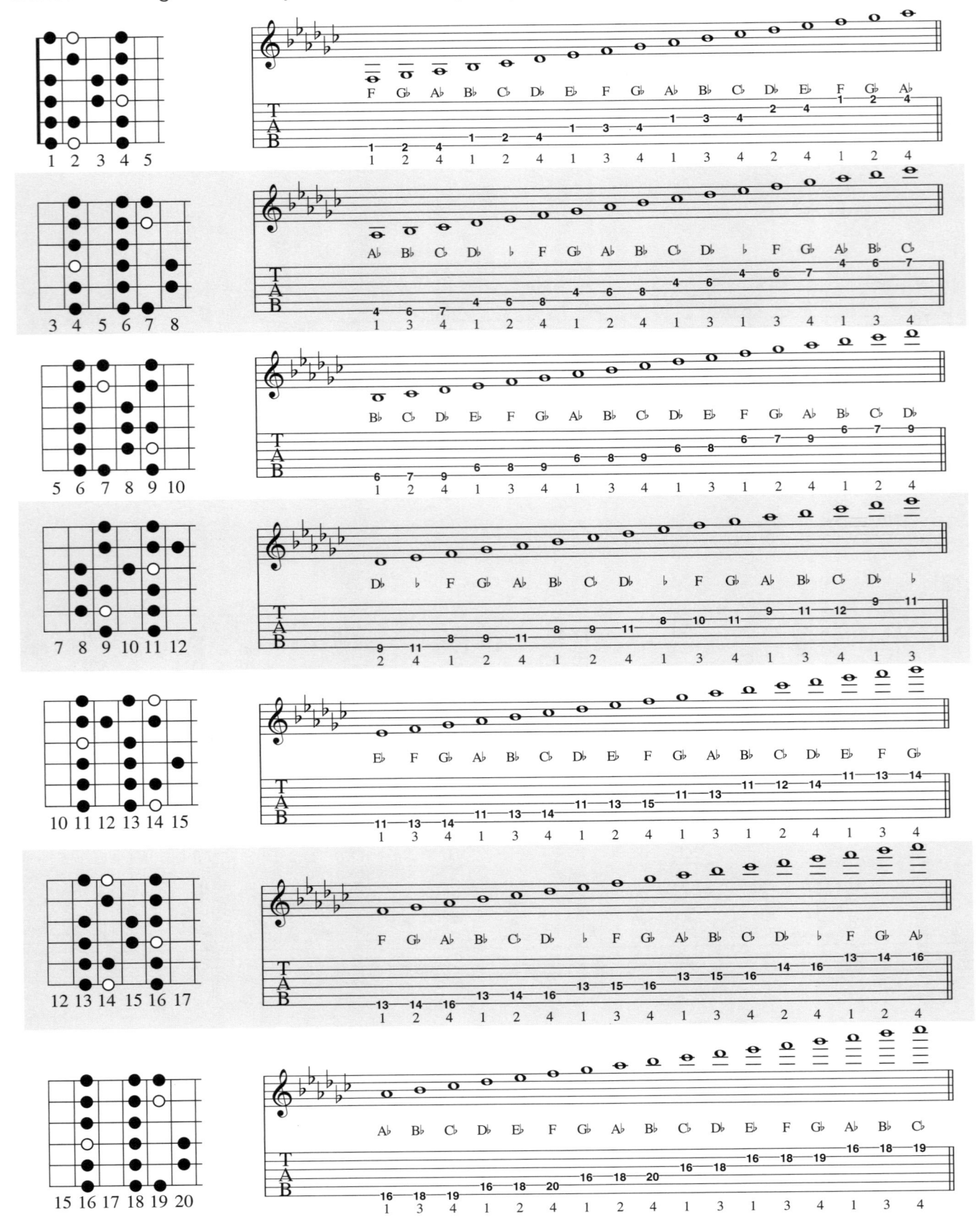

G♭ Major Exercises

EXAMPLE 15.1

Play in 1st position.

EXAMPLE 15.2

Play in 1st position.

EXAMPLE 15.3

Play in 4th, 6th and 8th positions.

Example 15.4
Play in 8th, 11th, 13th and 16th positions.

Example 15.5
Play in 8th position.

Example 15.6
Play in 8th, 11th, 13th and 16th positions.

Example 15.7
Play in 11th, 13th and 16th positions.

Example 15.8
Play in 13th and 16th positions.

Example 15.9
Play in 16th position.

G♭ Major Harmonic Reading Exercises

Examples 15.10–15.12 are in G♭ Major.

Example 15.10
Play in 4th, 6th and 8th positions.

Example 15.11
Play in 6th and 9th positions.

Example 15.12

Chapter 16—C# Major Reading Exercises

C# Major Scale Fingerings

The fretboard diagrams below show the positions for the C# Major scale based on the shapes you learned on page 20. The key of C# Major has seven sharps (F#, C#, G#, D#, A# and E#). Though C# Major is rarely used, it provides an excellent challenge for sight-reading practice.

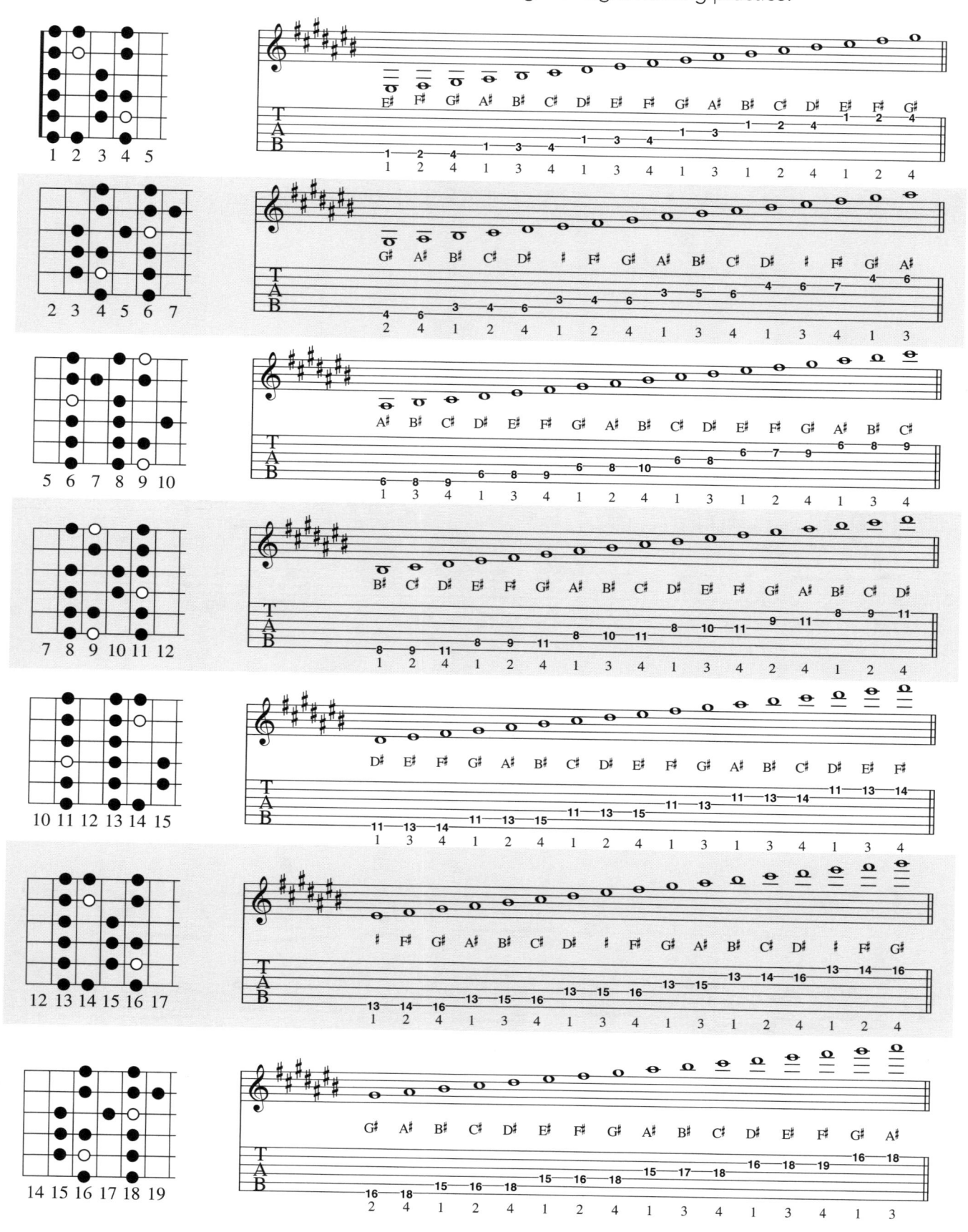

C# Major Exercises

Example 16.1
Play in 1st position.

Example 16.2
Play in 1st and 3rd positions.

Example 16.3
Play in 3rd position.

Sight-Reading for the Contemporary Guitarist 91

EXAMPLE 16.4

Play in 6th and 8th positions.

EXAMPLE 16.5

Play in 6th and 8th positions.

EXAMPLE 16.6

Play in 8th and 11th positions.

92 Sight-Reading for the Contemporary Guitarist

EXAMPLE **16.7**

Play in 8th and 11th positions.

EXAMPLE **16.8**

Play in 11th, 13th and 16th positions.

EXAMPLE **16.9**

Play in 16th position.

Sight-Reading for the Contemporary Guitarist

C# Major Harmonic Reading Exercises

Examples 16.10–16.12 are in C# Major. Don't forget to make *every* note a sharp.

Example 16.10
Play in 1st position.

Example 16.11
Play in 9th position.

Example 16.12

Chapter 17 – C♭ Major Reading Exercises

C♭ MAJOR SCALE POSITIONS

Congratulations! You've made it to C♭ Major, the last of our major keys. C♭ Major has seven flats (B♭, E♭, A♭, D♭, G♭, C♭ and F♭). Notice that these positions and those for B Major are essentially the same, since the two keys are enharmonically equivalent. But if you can sight-read well in C♭, you should be able to handle nearly any sight-reading situation you encounter.

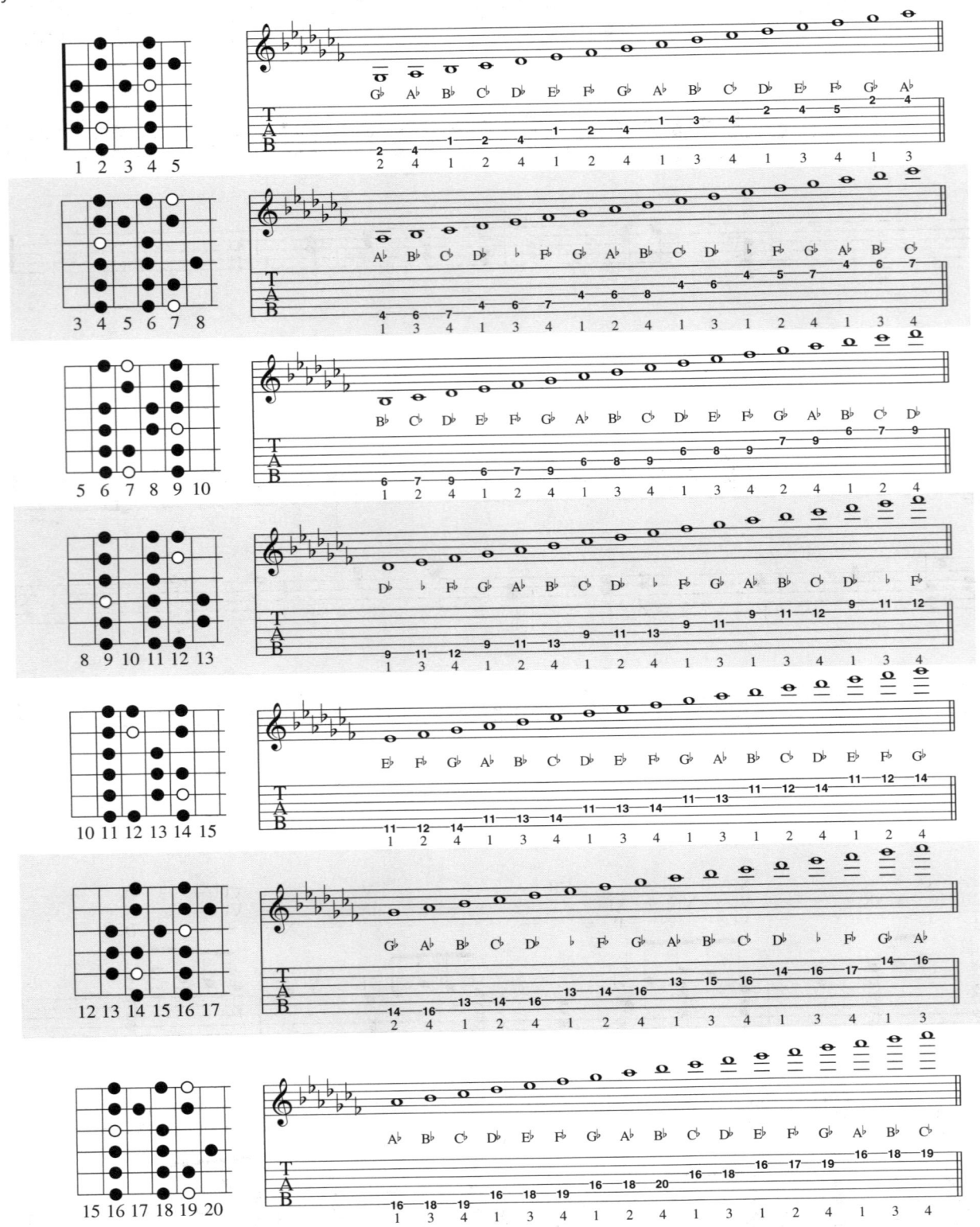

C♭ Major Exercises

Example 17.1

Play in 1st and 4th positions.

Example 17.2

Play in 1st, 4th, 6th and 8th positions.

Example 17.3

Play in 4th position.

96 Sight-Reading for the Contemporary Guitarist

Example 17.4
Play in 6th and 8th positions.

Example 17.5
Play in 8th, 11th and 13th positions.

Example 17.6
Play in 6th position.

Example 17.7

Play in 11th, 13th and 16th positions.

Example 17.8

Play in 11th position.

Example 17.9

Play in 16th position.

C♭ Major Harmonic Reading Exercises

As with the C♯ Major reading exercises in the previous chapter, Examples 17.10–17.12 may at first look as though they're in C Major. However, since they're in C♭ Major, just flat *every* note.

The next two harmonic exercises are best handled without an eye to staying in any particular position. You will need to move freely along the string to finger the intervals and chords.

Example 17.10

Example 17.11

Example 17.12

Chapter 18—More Multi-Position Reading

At this point, you've made it through basic training as a sight-reader, and you've become pretty familiar with playing in different positions in different keys. Now, we'll take on a new challenge: pieces that use *chromatic notes* (notes outside a given key), a less strongly defined key center, or more than one key center.

The examples in this chapter use the principles and positions you've learned so far. However, these examples also use an expanded musical vocabulary, and no single position will work throughout an entire example. The main goal for these examples is to deepen your familiarity with the notes throughout the fretboard. Begin by working out the different positions required for each exercise in one way, then start in a different location on the neck and take it from there. The more solutions you explore, the more fluent you'll be when it comes to finding positions as you sight-read.

EXAMPLE 18.1

Example 18.2

EXAMPLE 18.3

EXAMPLE 18.4

EXAMPLE 18.5

Chapter 19—Reading in Odd Time

The exercises in this chapter are designed to help you become more familiar and comfortable with sight-reading in *odd time* (also called *asymmetrical time*). While odd time can be explained in a number of ways, think of it in the most general terms: an unusual (most often odd) number of beats per measure. For example, while most of the music we play has 2, 3, 4, 6, 9 or 12 beats per measure, some music calls for 5 beats per measure, or 7 beats, or an even "odder" number. As you'll see in this chapter, one of the keys to playing in time signatures like $\frac{5}{4}$ or $\frac{7}{8}$ is thinking in terms of the smaller units that make up these "odd" numbers.

FIVE BEATS PER MEASURE

Odd time signatures work the same way as the time signatures you already know. The top number indicates the number of beats per measure, while the lower number indicates what note value receives 1 beat. For example, $\frac{5}{4}$ means that there are 5 beats in each measure, and each of these beats is equal to a quarter note. Measures of 5 beats are most often felt in one of three ways: as a single unit of 5, as a group of 3 plus a group of 2 (3 + 2), or as a group of 2 plus a group of 3.

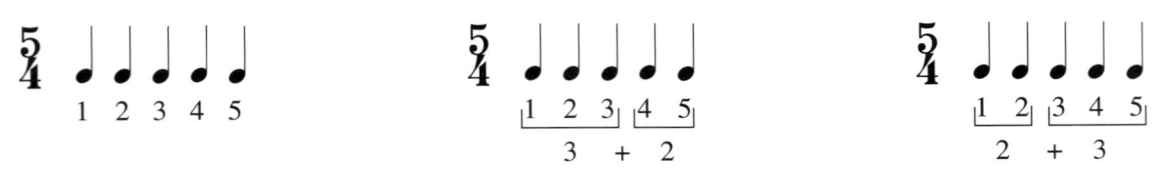

The most natural division of a measure in odd time is often apparent from the rhythms themselves. Sometimes, the feeling may change from one measure to the next. Example 19.1 is built on a pattern of 3 + 2. Play this example in 8th, 10th and 12th positions.

EXAMPLE 19.1

Example 19.2 is built on a pattern of 2 + 3. Play this example in 7th, 9th and 12th positions.

EXAMPLE 19.2

Example 19.3 uses a combination of 3 + 2 and 2 + 3. Play this example in 11th position.

EXAMPLE 19.3

SEVEN BEATS PER MEASURE

The principles that apply to $\frac{7}{4}$ are generally the same as those for $\frac{5}{4}$. In this case, there are seven beats per measure, which can be divided in a number of ways.

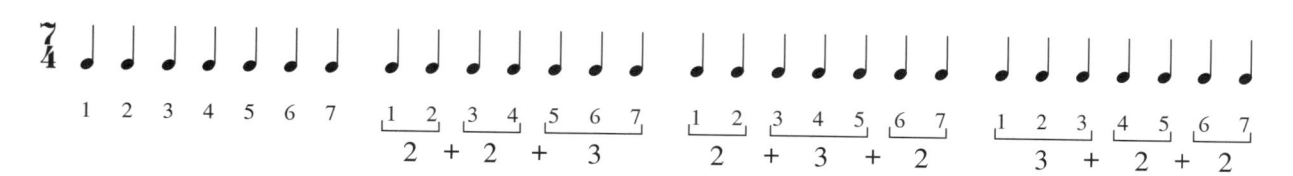

Examples 19.4 and 19.5 on page 106 demonstrate these different groupings.

Example 19.4 is based on a pattern of 3 + 2 + 2.

EXAMPLE 19.5

Example 19.5 uses a combination of 2 + 2 + 3, 2 + 3 + 2, and 3 + 2 + 2.

EXAMPLE 19.5

Chapter 20—Chord Chart Reading Exercises

While the sight-reading we've done so far has involved fully notated melodies, you may also be called on to sight-read chord charts. In most cases, this will simply involve applying chord shapes to a notated rhythmic line. For a review of commonly used chords and chord shapes, check out *Theory for the Contemporary Guitarist* by Guy Capuzzo and *Guitar Chord and Scale Finder* by Jody Fisher, both published by the National Guitar Workshop/Alfred Publishing.

Example 20.1

EXAMPLE 20.2

Example 20.3

Example 20.4

EXAMPLE 20.5

The Final Bar

Look at how far you've come. When you first picked up this book, you may have been at a point where you were still learning the location of different notes on the guitar. But now, more than 100 pages later, you're playing in all 12 major keys and moving all over the fretboard like nobody's business. You can play in any time signature known in the free world, and you can interpret any chord chart that's placed in front of you. You'll never again be the butt of another joke about how guitar players can't read music.

One thing is for sure: You're well on your way to real sight-reading mastery. Your sight-reading muscles are much stronger, but now you need to keep these muscles in shape by "increasing the weight"—sight-reading as much and as often as you can. Try using your sight-reading skills in new ways. Practice transposing by playing pieces an octave higher than written. Read ahead as you play. Stay focused on training your eyes, brain and hands to work in perfect harmony. If you continue to work on your sight-reading in this way, it will become a much more natural process—and you'll also broaden the breadth of your musical experiences. Thanks for spending this time with me. It is my sincere hope that we can one day sit down together and read some music.

See you on the bandstand.—*Tom Dempsey*

IF YOU ENJOYED THIS BOOK, YOU'LL LOVE OUR SCHOOL
NATIONAL GUITAR WORKSHOP

Guitar
Bass
Voice
Drums
Keyboards

Rock
Blues
Classical
Alternative
Songwriting
Acoustic
Country
Fusion
Jazz
Funk

1-800-234-6479
NGW • BOX 222 • LAKESIDE, CT 06758
Call or write for a free brochure.
www.guitarworkshop.com